for Six Sigma

MEMORY
JOGGER™

Tools and
Methods for
Robust
Processes
and Products

Dana Ginn
Oriel Incorporated

Evelyn Varner
Vital Statistics Incorporated

First Edition
GOAL/QPC

The Design for Six Sigma Memory Jogger™

Oriel, Inc.

Dana Ginn, *Writer*
Evelyn Varner, *Writer*
Barbara Streibel, *Content Expert*
Christine Jersild, *Project Manager*

GOAL/QPC

Daniel Picard, *Editor*
Michele Kierstead, *Cover Design, Graphics, and Layout*
Bob Page, *Project Manager*

GOAL/QPC

12B Manor Parkway, Salem, NH 03079-2862
Toll free: 800-643-4316 **or** 603-893-1944
Fax: 603-870-9122
E-mail: service@goalqpc.com
Web site: www.goalqpc.com

Printed in the United States of America
First Edition   10 9 8 7 6 5 4 3 2 1

ISBN 1-57681-047-X

Acknowledgments

Many thanks to all who offered encouragement and suggestions for this book and who gave us permission to use their examples and charts. In the truest sense, this has been a team effort.

Special thanks to Patricia Klossner and her team at Oriel, Incorporated who generously shared their time, knowledge, and experience, and to Larry Smith of Ford Motor Company who challenged us to create a book that meets the needs of both manufacturing and nonmanufacturing readers.

Thanks to the following reviewers whose suggestions helped to ensure that the finished book would meet their needs and expectations:

James Bossert, *Bank of America*; Kristi Spittler-Brown, *Wal-Mart Stores, Incorporated*; Michael S. Englund, *Honeywell, Incorporated*; Bruce K. Jankowski, *United States Surgical, Division of Tyco Healthcare Group LP*; Ian Osborn, *Maytag Corporation*; Jay P. Patel, *Quality & Productivity Solutions, Inc.*; Mary Beth Soloy, *Ford Motor Company*; David Speer, *Maytag Corporation*; Roger Stemen, *Raytheon Company*.

Foreword

At GOAL/QPC, we believe that Six Sigma is redefining the world of work and that organizations will need to incorporate the various Six Sigma methodologies into their training and education programs for current and future employees. Our main objective in developing *The Design for Six Sigma Memory Jogger*™ is to provide a quick reference guide for people who are tasked with designing (or redesigning) processes, products, and services at six sigma levels of performance and to enable them to perform that work well. We are assuming that the users of this book will be experienced in the basics of Six Sigma, thus allowing us to concentrate our resources on the DMADV (Define, Measure, Analyze, Design, and Verify) steps of the Design for Six Sigma process.

Our goal, in creating this book, is to:

- Provide a clear roadmap that champions, project leaders, and project team members can follow from project initiation to closeout.

- Create a means for all parties involved in design activities to know where they are at any given point in the evolution of the project.

- Provide resources for further study and greater proficiency in tools and methods that, due to space limitations, could not be covered in greater detail in this book.

We hope that this and our other Six Sigma products will help to provide the information that your employees need to successfully meet the demands of their customers and stakeholders.

Bob Page
Director of New Product Development
GOAL/QPC

Table of Contents

How to Use this Book

The Design for Six Sigma Memory Jogger™ is designed to be a learning and performance support resource that will help all members of your team understand the sequence of activities in the DMADV process and learn how to perform each step and substep in the process.

To achieve these objectives and help you understand how all of this information fits together, we have created a number of features for this book, including:

- A flowchart and unique numbering system for the major DMADV process steps and substeps. (The complete flowchart is shown in The DMADV Methodology chapter, and sections of the flowchart are shown again as each major step is introduced.)

- A matrix that describes the major steps, the tools used to execute the steps, and the major outputs of each step. (The matrix is also included as part of The DMADV Methodology chapter.)

The individual chapters of the book explain each of the DMADV process steps in detail. The tools you will use to complete each step or substep can be identified by a toolbox icon at the beginning of each tool section, and are set off from the text by a blue background, to make them easier to locate. (Tools that are "nested" within other tool sections are set off on a white background.)

In addition, the Appendix to this book includes:

- A resource section with text and web-based resources for many of the highly detailed, industry-specific tools that are, unfortunately, beyond the scope of this book.

- A sigma conversion chart, for quick reference.

- A section on Storyboards, for convenience.

We hope you find this information useful on your journey to excellence!

Six Sigma Overview

What is Six Sigma?

Sigma is a statistical concept that represents the amount of variation present in a process relative to customer requirements or specifications. The higher the sigma level, the better the process is performing relative to customer requirements.

Too much variation	Hard to produce output within customer requirements (specifications)	Low sigma values (0–2)
Moderate variation	Most output meets customer requirements	Middle sigma values (2–4.5)
Very little variation	Virtually all output meets customer requirements (less than 4 defects per million opportunities)	High sigma values (4.5–6)

To increase the sigma level of a process, you must decrease the amount of variation and make sure that the process is targeted appropriately. Decreased variation provides:

- Greater predictability in the process.
- Less waste and rework, which lowers costs.
- Products and services that perform better and last longer.
- Happier customers who value you as a supplier.

Estimates place the quality levels of key processes in successful businesses today within the three- to four-sigma range. But an entire world operating at a four-sigma level would incur:

- At least 20,000 wrong drug prescriptions dispensed per year.
- Ninety-six crashes per 100,000 airline flights.
- Unsafe drinking water for almost one hour each month.
- No telephone service or television transmission for nearly ten minutes each week.

However, when a process operates at a *six-sigma* level, the variation is so small that the resulting products and services are 99.9997% defect free. A world operating at a six-sigma level would be much safer, with far fewer errors than the ones listed above.

In addition to being a statistical measure of variation, the term *Six Sigma* also refers to a business philosophy that says an organization is committed to understanding and providing what its customers need, by analyzing and improving its business processes to meet those needs. The organization has set a level of six sigma (no more than 3.4 defects per million opportunities [DPMO]) as a quality goal for the products and services it provides to its customers.

Note: *Six Sigma* is commonly denoted in several different ways—as 6σ, *6 Sigma*, or *6s*. In this book, we will use the generic terms *sigma* or *process sigma* to refer to the current capability of a process (i.e., how well the process is performing relative to customer specifications).

Why should I use Six Sigma?

The many benefits of pursuing Six Sigma and using the accompanying methods include:

- Having a measurable way to track performance improvements.

- Focusing your attention on process management at all organizational levels.

- Improving your customer relationships by addressing defects.

- Improving the efficiency and effectiveness of your processes by aligning them with your customers' needs.

- Developing new processes, products, and services that meet critical customer requirements upon initial offering.

Two essential elements are implied in the definition of Six Sigma:

1. Understanding your organization's work from a *process viewpoint*, and

2. Clearly defining *customer requirements*

Process Viewpoint

To make changes that last, you must see your organization's work as the result of a series of interactive functions, operations, and methods called systems or processes. A process is a series of steps or tasks that converts an input into an output. Making an engine block, going on a sales call, filling a vacant position, or admitting a patient are all examples of processes. Processes apply to all work, whether repetitive in nature or "one-of-a-kind."

An Organization's Systems and Processes

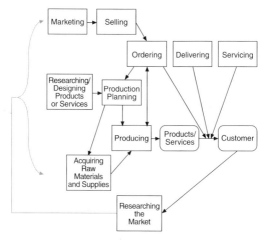

Note: "Researching the Market" will provide customer feedback that can impact any part of the system or process.

In this diagram, the rectangular boxes represent the core processes. Linked together, they illustrate the highest-level process view in the organization. These processes interact to provide products and services to the customer.

To improve the quality of products and services (i.e., increase the sigma level), you must improve the systems and processes involved.

Customer Requirements

Customer requirements in Six Sigma are generally referred to as Critical to Quality (CTQ) characteristics. CTQs are those features of your product or service that are critical from the perspective of your customers.

A CTQ should have:

- A quality characteristic that specifies how the product or service will meet the customer need.
- A quantitative measure for the performance of the quality characteristic.
- A target value that represents the desired level of performance that the characteristic should meet.
- Specification limits that define the performance limits that customers will tolerate.

Six Sigma methodologies

To achieve Six Sigma, a business must excel at managing existing processes (process management), improving existing processes (DMAIC), and designing new processes, products, and services (DMADV). Linking these three methodologies proves to be the most effective way for an organization to achieve its Six Sigma goals.

Linked Six Sigma Methodologies

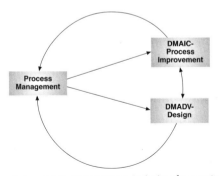

Ongoing process management includes the *monitoring and control of an organization's processes*. Process management is both a source for new improvement and design projects, and the system that supports and maintains the projects' solutions. (This system is needed to sustain and improve a new design once it is fully implemented.)

The Define-Measure-Analyze-Improve-Control (DMAIC) improvement process is used to *incrementally improve existing processes*. Improving an organization's processes will result in improved products and services.

DMAIC

The Define-Measure-Analyze-Design-Verify (DMADV) design process is used when a *new* process, product, or service is needed, or when an existing process, product, or service *requires such significant change* that an improvement process is inadequate.

DMADV

Both the DMAIC and the DMADV methodologies rely on a process viewpoint and an understanding of customer requirements.

©2004 GOAL/QPC

Because *DMAIC* improves what currently exists, the Voice of the Customer work (i.e., the customer needs and perceptions) in DMAIC usually focuses on understanding the reasons the process, product, or service cannot consistently meet a key customer requirement. *DMADV*, on the other hand, usually involves substantially more work obtaining and analyzing the Voice of the Customer so that the process, product, or service is designed to meet multiple customer requirements from the outset.

DMAIC and DMADV Methodologies

DMAIC

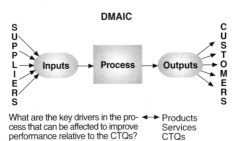

What are the key drivers in the process that can be affected to improve performance relative to the CTQs? ← → Products Services CTQs

DMADV

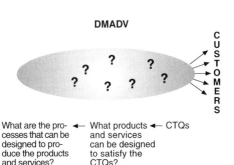

What are the processes that can be designed to produce the products and services? ← What products and services can be designed to satisfy the CTQs? ← CTQs

Although some of the DMAIC and DMADV methodology steps have similar names, there are distinct differences in the purpose of the steps and in the tools used.

DMAIC vs. DMADV

DMAIC	DMADV
Define the project: • Develop a clear definition of the project. • Collect background information on the current process and your customers' needs and requirements.	**Define** the project: • Develop a clear definition of the project. • Develop organizational change plans, risk management plans, and project plans.
Measure the current situation: • Gather information on the current situation to provide a clearer focus for your improvement effort.	**Measure** customer requirements: • Collect the Voice of the Customer (VOC) data. • Translate the VOC into design requirements (CTQs). • Identify the most important CTQs. • Develop a phased approach if necessary.
Analyze to identify causes: • Identify the root causes of defects. • Confirm them with data.	**Analyze** concepts: • Generate, evaluate, and select the concept that best meets the CTQs within budget and resource restraints.
Improve: • Develop, test, and implement solutions that address the root causes. • Use data to evaluate results for the solutions and the plans used to carry them out.	**Design:** • Develop the high-level and detailed design. • Test the design components. • Prepare for pilot and full-scale deployment.

Continued on next page

DMAIC	DMADV
Control: • Maintain the gains that you have achieved by standardizing your work methods or processes. • Anticipate future improvements and make plans to preserve the lessons learned from this improvement effort.	**Verify** design performance: • Conduct the pilot, and stress-test and debug the prototype. • Implement the design. • Transition responsibility to the appropriate people in the organization. • Close the team.

Why should I use DMADV?

There are reasons why an organization would want to apply DMADV instead of DMAIC:

- To design processes, products, and services that do not currently exist

- To improve an existing process, product, or service if:

  - It is not designed for current capacity

  - It fails to meet multiple customer requirements

  - There are multiple fundamentally different versions in use

  - The organization cannot improve the process, product, or service using the existing technology, as evidenced by repeated unsuccessful improvement attempts

People tend to differentiate between product and service designs. However, black-and-white distinctions between products and services are not meaningful in practice. The output of most industries is a mixture of both. For example, a service industry such as banking has associated physical products (e.g., an ATM) whose quality is an integral part of the service experience.

Customers do not make distinctions between the product and service aspects of an organization; customers view the outputs of a company as a package, and the total performance of the elements of the package determines the degree of customer satisfaction. By focusing explicitly and systematically on customer needs, the DMADV methodology supports the design of all of the elements that are needed to delight customers.

DMADV allows an organization to *refocus on the customer requirements*, ensuring greater accuracy and reduced variation about the target in a way that can provide dramatic results and high sigma levels from the outset.

It is generally accepted that the DMAIC methodology can shift a sigma level from 3 sigma to about 5.0–5.5 sigma. At that point, the rate of return on effort diminishes considerably. For this reason, continued use of the DMAIC methodology may be inadequate. To achieve higher sigma performance, you must *redesign* the process, product, or service so that the *design itself* will ensure the capability of achieving a higher level of performance.

DMADV does require a significant time and effort investment up front, but in the long term, it is much more cost-efficient because you do not incur the costs to correct problems after you introduce a new process, product, or service. The typical post-release activity represents fixes and redesigns that are necessary to repair the original design as it moves into full implementation. The DMADV methodology minimizes this crisis activity by delivering processes, products, and services that are more likely to meet customer and business requirements from the initial launch.

---

10 Six Sigma Overview ©2004 GOAL/QPC

DMADV Reduces Typical Post-Release Activities

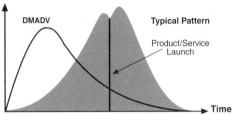

Projects that use the DMADV methodology use fewer resources and use them up front. This can be challenging to many organizations because key resources are requested when there is no crisis and these organizations are accustomed to doing the first stages of projects with less investment.

Deciding between DMAIC and DMADV projects

Regardless of whether an organization begins with DMAIC or with DMADV, project generation and selection are critical steps *prior* to initiating the improvement or design cycles.

Use the Flowchart on the next page when initiating projects to determine whether the project should follow a DMAIC or a DMADV path.

Should I Use DMAIC or DMADV?

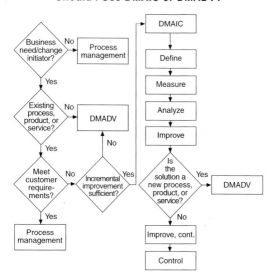

What are the roles and responsibilities associated with a DMADV project?

Each DMADV project requires a coordinated effort among many people.

Senior business leaders or champions identify objectives for the organization's processes, products, and services based on the organization's strategic plans. Depending on how well the current processes, products, and services perform, champions identify which existing processes, products, or services need improvement, and which new processes, products, or services need to be designed.

©2004 GOAL/QPC

Six Sigma Roles

There are five major roles in a DMADV project. Their primary responsibilities are explained on the following pages.

Champions

- Select key areas for change
- Select design projects that are linked to the strategic direction and business needs
- Identify the design team sponsor
- Identify the process owner and ensure his/her appropriate involvement in the project
- Manage the project "pipeline"
- Approve charters
- Coordinate/integrate projects
- Review progress
- Approve recommended solutions and funding
- Ensure that management systems can maintain the gains across the business
- Recognize and communicate efforts

Project Sponsor

- Selects the coach and team leader
- Drafts the team charter
- Provides needed resources
- Selects team members with the team leader
- Collaborates with the team leader to orient the team to the project
- Reviews team progress frequently
- Provides guidance, direction, and support
- Intervenes to remove barriers to success
- Monitors other initiatives for overlap/conflicts
- Helps transition responsibility from the team to the organization during implementation and ongoing monitoring

- Informs the champions' group and others of progress/learnings
- Ensures that recommended changes are implemented
- Ensures that project results are quantified and documented
- Ensures continued monitoring of key processes, measures, and solutions
- Preserves and uses the lessons learned
- Celebrates the team's accomplishments

Coach (often referred to as the Master Black Belt or Quality Advisor)

- Develops team leaders
- Facilitates team success
- Provides design and statistical/technical expertise
- Coaches sponsors and process owners

Team Leader (often referred to as the Black Belt)

- Is responsible for the project's progress and planning the team's work
- Communicates to the project sponsor and management team
- Develops, updates, and manages all project plans
- Does the project work, in conjunction with team members

Team Member

- Supplies necessary technical expertise and does the project work
- Works collaboratively with others to develop, test, and implement the design
- Leads sub-teams (as necessary) during some phases of the design

Sources for DMADV Projects

There are many potential sources for DMADV projects. These include, but are not limited to:

- New opportunities created by a research or development breakthrough.

- A need to respond to a competitor's move.

- A desire to leapfrog the competition and gain competitive advantage.

- The implementation of regulatory/certification requirements.

- A need to meet new customer requirements.

There are basically two ways to initiate DMADV projects. The first is to have the business strategy initiate projects directly. For example, design efforts can result from identifying new markets or market segments to target, deciding to offer new products or services to existing customers to maintain their loyalty, or reframing the business purpose (e.g., moving from a "cash register" company to a "business solutions" company).

A second source of DMADV projects is through improvement projects that, after analyzing the underlying cause/effect relationships responsible for customer unhappiness, demonstrate that improving existing processes, products, or services will not meet customer requirements. A new design is needed.

Regardless of how it is initiated, a DMADV project should begin with information about how it is expected to contribute to the business strategy and the market or customer requirements it is intended to address.

Choosing a collection of projects is quite similar to managing an investment portfolio. In both cases you need to:

- Balance solid, smaller payback with riskier high returns.
- Balance short-term and long-term gain.
- Address the diversity of strategic issues.

How do I select DMADV projects?

Select projects that will have the greatest impact on the business strategy, key performance indicators, and critical customer requirements. Then communicate the project in a way that clearly describes the link between the project and the strategic priorities of the company, and that describes how the benefits of the project will be measured.

Project Selection Process

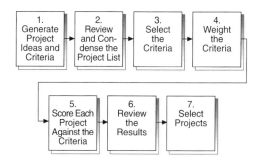

To select DMADV projects:

1. **Generate project ideas and criteria based on the business issues.**

   • Consider:

      - The organization's strategic direction.

      - Customer information.

      - Competitive, industry, and benchmarking trends and data.

      - Current management dashboards and other measures.

      - Current bottlenecks to success.

      - Other related data from the business, employees, and marketplace. To uncover this data, ask:

         a) What new products, services, or other capabilities can we create to provide increased value to our customers and shareholders?

         b) Which processes are the most expensive? Which are the most cumbersome?

         c) What barriers exist that prevent us from increasing customer satisfaction?

         d) What new needs are on the horizon for our customers? How can we better anticipate those needs?

         e) What concerns or ideas have employees raised?

2. **Review and combine the project list that you develop with any existing project lists.**

3. **Select criteria to use in further condensing the project list.**

   • Consider:

      - Clear links to the business strategy.

      - The resources available to allocate.

- The potential high impact to profitability through increased revenues and/or reduced costs.
- The availability of customer data or the relative ease to collect this data.
- The potential for the project to significantly increase process performance.
- The ability of the project sponsor to commit time and resources.
- The funding available for solutions.
- A manageable time frame (generally, 6–12 months; longer design projects can be handled in six-month phases).

4. **Weight the criteria.**
5. **Score each potential project against the criteria.**
6. **Review the results to ensure that they make sense.**
   • Identify and reconcile any inconsistencies.
7. **Select the initial projects.**

What do I need for a successful DMADV program?

Your DMADV initiative will only be successful if your organization's culture supports its continued and consistent use. To accomplish this, your organization should:

• Have management lead your improvement efforts.

• Actively support a focus on delighting your customers.

• Provide the DMADV project team with access to experts who can offer ongoing guidance and coaching.

- Encourage open discussion about defects. (People should not be afraid to point out that something is wrong. The airline industry, for instance, studies crashes and "near-misses" to improve safety.)

- Value and use the data you gather.

- Help employees work effectively by providing a team-based, cooperative environment.

The DMADV Methodology

What is the DMADV methodology?

DMADV is a five-step method for designing new processes, products, or services, or completely redesigning ones that already exist. The flowchart on the next page shows the five steps and their associated substeps. (Each step is explained in greater detail in subsequent chapters of this book.)

> **Tip** Although the process appears linear and there is a specific order to the work (e.g., you gather information on customer needs before generating concepts, and you work at the concept level before attempting to design the details), there are also a lot of recurring actions within the design process. For example, you will start to gather customer requirements as part of the Measure step, but will continue to deepen your understanding of customer requirements throughout the Analyze and Design steps.

Note: In this book, the steps and substeps of the DMADV process are sequentially numbered to serve as a navigational aid. As you read this book, use this numbering system and the linear DMADV methodology flowchart to quickly orient yourself to your current position in the process.

Each step of the DMADV method uses specific tools that generate specific outputs, as detailed in the chart at the end of this chapter.

The DMADV Methodology

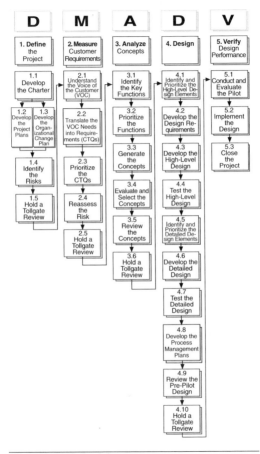

©2004 GOAL/QPC

Steps	Tools	Outputs
1. Define the project: • Develop a clear definition of the project. • Develop organizational change plans, risk management plans, and project plans.	• Market analysis tools: - Market forecasting tools - Customer value analysis - Technology forecasting and visioning - Competitor analysis • Process analysis tools: - Control charts - Pareto charts • Traditional project planning tools: - Work breakdown structures - PERT charts - Gantt charts - Activity network diagrams • DMADV-specific tools: - Project charter - In-scope/out-of-scope tool - Organizational change plan	• Project charter • Project plan • Organizational change plan • Risk management plan • Tollgate review and Storyboard presentation
2. Measure customer requirements: • Collect the Voice of the Customer (VOC) data. • Translate the VOC into design requirements (CTQs). • Identify the most important CTQs. • Revise the risk management plan. • If necessary, develop a multistage project plan.	• Customer segmentation tree • Data collection plan • Customer research tools: - Interviews - Contextual inquiry - Focus groups - Surveys • VOC table • Affinity diagrams • Kano model • Performance benchmarking • Quality function deployment (QFD) matrix • CTQ risk matrix • Multistage plan • Tollgate review form	• Prioritized CTQs • Updated risk management plan and multistage project plan, if appropriate • Tollgate review and updated Storyboard

Steps	Tools	Outputs

3. Analyze concepts:
• Generate, evaluate, and select the concept that best meets the CTQs within budget and resource constraints.
	• QFD matrix
	• Creativity tools:
	  - Brainstorming/ Brainwriting
	  - Analogies
	  - Assumption busting
	  - Morphological box
	• Pugh matrix
	• Tollgate review forms
		• Selected concept for further analysis and design
		• Tollgate review and updated Storyboard

4. Design: • Develop the high-level and detailed design. • Test the design components. • Prepare for pilot and full-scale deployment.	• QFD matrix • Simulation • Prototyping • Design scorecard • FMEA/EMEA • Planning tools • Process management chart • Tollgate review forms	• Tested and approved high-level design • Tested and approved detailed design • Detailed, updated risk assessment • Plans for conducting the pilot • Completed design reviews and approvals • Tollgate review and updated Storyboard

5. Verify design performance:
• Conduct the pilot and stress-test and debug the prototype.
• Implement the design.
• Transition responsibility to the appropriate people in the organization.
• Close the team.
	• Planning tools
	• Data analysis tools:
	  - Control charts
	  - Pareto charts
	• Standardization tools:
	  - Flowcharts
	  - Checklists
	  - Process management charts
		• Working prototype with documentation
		• Plans for full implementation
		• Control plans to help process owners measure, monitor, and maintain process capability
		• Transition of ownership to operations
		• Completed project documentation
		• Project closure
		• Final tollgate review and updated Storyboard

Define

Customer Requirements

M
A
D
V

Why do it?

To develop a clear definition of the project that includes project plans, risk management plans, and organizational change plans. Projects that do not define their objectives, assign roles and responsibilities, and develop a project plan at this point in time often return to the Define step at a later date. This causes delays, disillusions teams, and generally threatens a project's viability.

Tools used in this step:

- Market analysis tools:
  - Market forecasting tools
  - Customer value analysis
  - Technology forecasting and visioning
  - Competitor analysis
- Process analysis tools:
  - Control charts
  - Pareto charts
- Traditional project planning tools:
  - Work breakdown structures
  - PERT charts
  - Gantt charts
  - Activity Network Diagrams

- DMADV-specific tools:
  - The project charter
  - The In-Scope/Out-of-Scope Tool
  - The organizational change plan
  - Risk management plans
  - Tollgate Review Forms

Note: Market analysis tools are beyond the scope of this book. Process analysis tools are explained in *The Six Sigma Memory Jogger™ II*. Traditional project planning tools are highlighted here and can be referenced in more detail in *The Six Sigma Memory Jogger™ II* and the *Project Management Memory Jogger™*.

Outputs of this step:
- A project charter
- A project plan
- An organizational change plan
- A risk management plan
- A tollgate review and Storyboard presentation

Key questions answered in this step:
- What are the strategic drivers for the project?
- What is the problem or opportunity we are trying to address?
- Why is improvement or the Plan-Do-Check-Act (PDCA) Cycle not adequate?
- What is the scope of the project?
- What is the project timeline and completion date?
- What team resources are needed?

©2004 GOAL/QPC

- What are the major risks associated with the project? When and how will we address those risks?

- How can we make sure the organization embraces and supports the changes resulting from the design?

How do I do it?

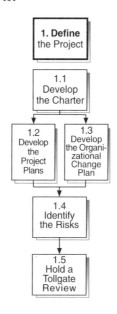

1.1 Develop the Charter

Charter

What is it?

The charter is an agreement between the champion team and your design team about what is expected of the project. The charter goes through several rounds of discussion as the project sponsor and the design team clarify uncertainties in definition and expectations. When the sponsor and the design team reach an agreement, the sponsor presents the charter to the champion team and facilitates communication between senior leadership and the design team.

Note: The charter will continue to evolve as the project unfolds and will need to be reviewed and updated periodically.

Why use it?

- To clarify what is expected of your design team and the design project before proceeding further

- To keep your team focused and aligned with organizational priorities

- To transfer the project from the champion team and sponsor(s) to the design team

How do I do it?

1. **Define the problem statement.**

- Describe the current situation and what is triggering the need for the design. Also describe the problems or challenges that internal and external customers experience, by addressing:

- What is wrong or not working?

- When and where do problems occur?

- How extensive are the problems?

- What is the impact on our customers, our business, and our employees?

- What will be the impact of changes in the market or business?

2. Create an opportunity statement.

- Describe the market opportunity that the new process, product, or service would address and the potential financial opportunity to which it could lead. Ask:

  - Who are the intended customers?

  - If we address this problem or issue, what benefit or value is added?

  - Will current customers increase their purchases?

  - Will addressing the problem or issue allow us to expand existing market segments or acquire new segments?

  - Will new customers begin to purchase from us?

  - Will customers purchase higher-margin products or services?

  - If we decrease costs, can we gain market share by passing the cost savings on to customers?

Tip If the DMADV project is focused on a new market opportunity instead of a problem to be fixed, then the opportunity statement becomes a more important part of the charter than the problem statement.

3. Define the importance of the project.

- Address the questions:
  - Why do this project now?
  - How does the project connect to the organization's short-term and long-term business strategies and/or objectives?
  - What is the larger picture that this project is part of?
  - How does this project contribute to the mission of the organization?

4. List the expectations/deliverables.

- Define the gap that the design will fill when completed. Define what you need to design, but do not specifically describe the process, product, or service that you will develop. Ask:
  - What will be the outcome of the design project?
  - What are the key elements (e.g., processes, information systems, technologies, people) that the design needs to address?
  - How will we know when the design is complete?
  - How will we know that the design is successful (e.g., by measuring target defect rates, margin improvements, customer satisfaction targets, or revenue growth)?

5. Determine the project scope.

- Determine what aspects of the process, product, or service the design will address, and ask:
  - What are the boundaries (starting and ending points) of the initiative?
  - What parts of the business are included?
  - What parts of the business are not included?

- What, if anything, is outside of the team's boundaries?

- What constraints (e.g.,no external resources, use existing technologies, etc.) do we need to work within?

- What are the nonnegotiables (e.g., time to market, etc.)?

Tip When drafting the charter, define the scope as well as possible given the information available at that point in the project. You will refine the scope in subsequent steps.

• Use the In-Scope/Out-of-Scope Tool to help you define the boundaries of the project.

What is it?
The In-Scope/Out-of-Scope Tool is a graphical method that clarifies the project's scope.

Why use it?
To help the team clarify which elements are within the boundaries of the project.

How do I do it?
1. **Brainstorm the elements of the project.**

   • Write each element on a separate Post-it® Note.

2. **Draw a circle on a flipchart to indicate the project's boundaries.**

---

3. Place the notes on the flipchart.

- Put the note inside the circle if the element is within the project's scope.
- Put the note outside the circle if the element is not within the project's scope.
- Put the note on the boundary of the circle if you are not sure if the element is within or outside the project's scope. Discuss any such items with the project sponsor.

4. Review the chart with the sponsor.

An In-Scope/Out-of-Scope Tool Example

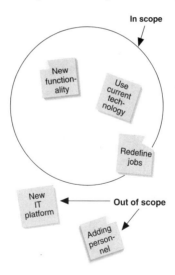

6. Create a project schedule.

• Include key milestones and the target dates for the completion of major steps in the project. Ask:

- What are the critical milestones for the project?

- What deadlines must we meet and why?

- What reviews should we schedule and when?

- What other business constraints must we take into account in scheduling the project?

• Focus on the key dates when deliverables are expected from the team. These dates will be estimates when you initially charter the project and may change when you learn more as the project progresses. Update the key dates and discuss these dates during project reviews.

Note: Design projects are usually very complex and often involve several teams working concurrently on different parts of the design during the latter steps in the process. Therefore, tracking progress against the plan for these projects usually requires excellent project management skills and project management software.

7. List the team resources.

• Identify the resources available to the team for specific tasks or specific periods of time. Answer:

- Who are the team members? Who is the team leader? Sponsor(s)? Key stakeholders? Other subject matter experts? What are their responsibilities?

- Which business functions or areas of expertise do we need? At what stage will we need them?

- How much time can each person devote to this project? How will their regular work be handled while they are on this project?

- What is the project structure? Who is accountable to whom and for what?

- How is the project linked to line management? What review structures are in place?

• Choose team leaders who have excellent project management skills, strong data analysis skills, knowledge of and experience in leading process improvements, and an ability to achieve results.

• Because design projects are often complex, cross-functional (sometimes cross-business), and critical to achieving business strategies, select sponsors who possess the skills and authority to mobilize resources, address barriers and conflicts, guide the team, and champion the project.

• When chartering the team, ensure that the initial core team represents all of the functions and areas of expertise that the project needs during the initial stages. After you choose a design concept, you may need to change the team's composition and add people to the design team. Make sure the team leader and coach are well-trained and experienced.

Tip Ensuring that design teams have all key functions and skills represented on the core team is critical to their success. Check the team composition for cross-functional representation, key skill areas, and experience levels. (For example, a team may need members from engineering, information technology, risk management, legal, finance, marketing, sales, and distribution departments.) In addition to including key skills on the team, create a team that blends both experience and new ideas, and include members who represent diverse perspectives. Review team membership at the end of each phase in the design

---

process; add or change members as needed for the work in the upcoming phase.

Tip Discuss who will be responsible for key tasks and how the team expects to work together before the project gets underway. This process, called role contracting, sets clear expectations and prevents misunderstandings and conflicts.

Use the following questions to help reach agreements about how the sponsor, team leader, coach, and team will work together:

• When should the team go to the sponsor for approval?

• When should the team and sponsor review progress? What is the coach's role in the reviews? Who has which responsibilities for the reviews?

• What topics should the team leader and sponsor discuss between reviews? Who should structure these meetings?

• How should the coach work with the sponsor? With the team leader? With the team?

Be sure to document these conversations to ensure clarity throughout the project.

A champion group usually selects the design projects and a project sponsor oversees the project. The project sponsor selects the team leader and drafts an initial charter, perhaps with input from the team leader. The team then discusses the charter, adding data, clarifying the charter elements, and noting any necessary revisions given their understanding of the project, its scope, and its customers. The team submits the revised charter to the sponsor for further discussion and approval.

Responsibilities When Developing a Charter

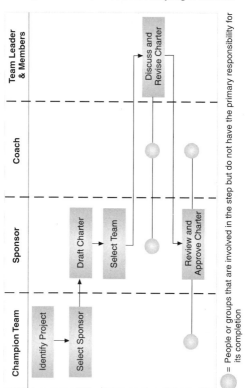

= People or groups that are involved in the step but do not have the primary responsibility for its completion

Team Leader & Members
- Discuss and Revise Charter

Coach

Sponsor
- Draft Charter
- Select Team
- Review and Approve Charter

Champion Team
- Identify Project
- Select Sponsor

A Sample Project Charter for Defining a Process or Service

Problem Statement:

As customers become more mobile, they have a growing need to place orders at any time, from any place, and through any channel. Our current order placement facility is unable to meet this need.

Opportunity Statement:

Over 50% of customers have access to more than one ordering channel. Studies have shown that this is the case for our competitors' customers as well. Providing flexible, multichannel access allows us to delight our own customers and gives us a significant competitive advantage over the current capabilities of our competitors.

Importance:

Multichannel ordering is currently gaining significant attention in the business world, and is the topic of many well-attended seminars and conferences. Speed of entry into this area will be a critical determinant of competitive advantage.

Expectations/Deliverables:

Design and build the processes, systems, and human resources needed to support flexible, multichannel ordering.

Scope:

The processes to be developed start when a customer places an order. The end point is when the order is transmitted into the production system and the customer receives confirmation. Orders are limited to domestic finished products and do not include direct orders for raw materials.

Project Schedule:

The overall project needs to be completed no later than 8/30.

- Define step by 2/15
- Measure step by 4/1
- Analyze step by 5/1
- Design step by 7/1
- Verify step by 8/25

Team Resources:

Julie	Sponsor	Eric	Coach
Beth	Team Leader	Pete	Information Technology
Sara	Sales		
Jack	Operations	Jan	Marketing
Betty	Finance	Luis	Production

Tip Be sure to spend sufficient time discussing and clarifying the charter elements to ensure that all team members, sponsors, and stakeholders understand the project's focus and scope. The initial charter should utilize whatever relevant data is available at the time. Remember that the charter is a living document that you will revise as you gather and analyze new data as the project progresses.

1.1 Develop the Project Plan

What is it?

The project plan is a detailed description of the project schedule and milestones. The plan includes an organizational change plan, a risk management plan, and a review schedule.

Why use it?

• To organize your team's daily activities (at the most detailed level)

• To help management review schedules and deadlines (at a task summary level)

• To allow an executive review of progress across projects (at the milestone level)

How do I do it?

1. **Integrate DMADV with your organization's related established processes.**

• Design projects often need to be integrated with other standard organizational processes (e.g., an existing product development or software development process). Spending time with others in the organization at the beginning of the project to integrate the project plan into those existing systems is usually well worth the effort because it may identify additional tasks that you will need to include in the project plan.

2. Develop the project schedule.

a) Start with important milestones. Milestones represent important decision points. The completion of each step in the design process is usually one of the milestones.

- Use the expertise of the entire team to define milestones. Ideally, you should have 10–15 milestones.

b) Organize the milestones into a logical sequence.

- Use tools such as Gantt charts, PERT charts, or Activity Network Diagrams to show the relationships between the milestones, define the critical path (i.e., the path of connected activities that shows the quickest possible implementation time), and build your project schedule.

c) Develop a detailed task structure.

- List the activities that must be completed in the project. Include:
  - Work tasks.
  - Coordination activities.
  - Communication activities.
  - Meetings.
  - Status reports and schedule reviews.
  - Design reviews.
  - Tollgate reviews.

d) Establish the task relationships.

- Ask:
  - What inputs does this activity require and where do they come from?
  - Does this activity produce any outputs that are required in another activity?
  - What activities must be completed so that this activity can be completed?
  - Where or how are the outputs of this activity used?
  - Can any activity be completed independently of other activities?

Tip When thinking about the relationships between the tasks, identify which activities must be completed before other tasks can begin, and which tasks cannot start until other tasks have begun. Determine how long each task will take (actual work time) and over what period of time (elapsed time). Identify the resources for each task to enable people to coordinate their work schedules.

e) Identify the critical path.

- Use the expertise of the entire team to establish dates for milestones. To estimate the target date for each milestone:
  - Estimate the tasks needed to reach each milestone.
  - Estimate the actual work time required for each task.
  - Estimate the resources available for each task.
  - Take into account factors such as time off, overtime required, learning curves, meetings, and time for consensus building.
  - Understand the relationships between the tasks needed to accomplish each milestone.

---

40 Define

- Use this information to determine the total duration time for each task and the overall project timeline.

A Sample Critical Path Matrix

Activity	Predecessors		Early		Late		Total Slack
			Start	Finish	Start	Finish	
A. Reporting relationships determined and documented		5 Days	3/4	3/10	3/4	3/10	0
B. Detailed office layouts completed	A	5 Days	3/11	3/17	3/11	3/17	0
C. Equipment needs identified	B	15 Days	3/18	4/7	3/18	4/7	0
D. Equipment ordered and received	C	25 Days	4/8	5/12	4/8	5/12	0
E. Installation of telephone/fax lines complete	C	5 Days	4/8	4/14	4/22	4/28	10
F. Installation of computer network complete	E	10 Days	4/15	4/28	4/29	5/12	10
G. Furniture needs identified	B	5 Days	3/18	3/24	4/8	4/14	15
H. Furniture ordered and received	G	20 Days	3/25	4/21	4/15	5/12	15
I. Equipment moved and installed	D,F,H	5 Days	5/13	5/19	5/13	5/19	0
J. Personal items moved	I	5 Days	5/20	5/26	5/20	5/25	0

You can also use a Gantt chart to summarize the flow of tasks across a timeline.

A Sample Gantt Chart

ID	Task name	Sep.	Qtr 4 Oct.	Qtr 4 Nov.	Qtr 4 Dec.	Qtr 1 Jan.	Qtr 1 Feb.	Qtr 1 Mar.	Qtr 2 Apr.	Qtr 2 May	Qtr 2 Jun.	Qtr 3 Jul.	Qtr 3 Aug.	Qtr 3 Sep.
1	ID customers		▮											
2	ID needs			▮										
3	ID CTQs			▮										
4	Review			▮										
5	Develop concepts				▮									
6	High-level design				▮									
7	Capability					▮								
8	Design review					▮								
9	Develop details						▮							
10	Simulation										▮			
11	Cost analysis									▮				
12	Design review											▮		
13	Procurement								▮					
14	Implementation													▮

Tip Design projects often have very complex task relationships because many concurrent activities occur simultaneously. Use a "rolling horizon" approach to develop detailed plans (i.e., create detailed plans for work to be done about four weeks out from the work currently being completed). The work that is further in the future can be left at a less-detailed level for now. Use a work breakdown structure (i.e., group the project tasks into a hierarchy that organizes and defines the total project work) to help you develop the task structure.

3. **Develop project management controls.**

- Identify the controls that protect the most vulnerable aspects of your project. Good project controls should:

  - Match the needs of the project.

  - Focus on a few key items.

  - Be reviewed and agreed upon by the team.

  - Be tested and understood before they are needed.

  Project controls ensure that planned events occur as planned, and unplanned events don't occur. All complex projects need project controls, but what the controls will focus on varies with the project. (For example, some projects may need safety and environmental controls while others need controls for work practices and ethical conduct.) The projects most in need of control mechanisms are those that involve a lot of people, over a long period of time, designing high reliability products or services.

- Be sure to match the controls to the project needs. Make them as simple and easy to use as possible. Make sure the benefits of the controls are understood so that everyone will support their use.

One example of a control mechanism is an issues board. An issues board lists the top 10–20 issues or problems associated with a project. Each issue is color-coded (green = "under control," yellow = "help needed," and red = "emergency"). The issues board is updated regularly (often daily) and also lists the person responsible for addressing the issue and the number of days the item has been on the list.

Category	Issue	Lead Person	Days Open
🔴 Red	Need customer data from potential markets	Luis	15
🟢 Green	Reschedule tollgate review	Jan	2
🟡 Yellow	Get cost/benefit data from Chief Financial Officer	Beth	4

4. **Control the project documentation.**

• Develop a method for organizing your project documents. If your organization already has a document management system, use it for your design project.

Document control is critical to control and manage the design changes while the sub-teams work concurrently. Document control should include:

• A central storage area (with a backup) to ensure centralized document retention.

• A date of creation and a version number on each document.

• Documents in the storage area that are accessible, but not available for modification.

Because documents change many times during a project, version control is an important issue. Find an easy way for team members, sponsors, and stake-holders to locate the most current version of all documents. Develop methods to review proposed changes in the documentation and to make approved changes in all relevant related documents.

1.3 Develop the Organizational Change Plan

What is it?

An organizational change plan ensures that the organization is prepared to support the project. The plan includes various change readiness assessment maps and communication plans.

Why use it?

To ensure that resources will be available and willing to help when needed. The organizational change plan will show who the change will impact and when their support will be needed in the project cycle.

Change is difficult for many people because the "way things are" is comfortable and often is part of their identity. To help people let go of the way things are and become supporters of the change, be sure to:

• Communicate vividly why things must change (e.g., customer demands/dissatisfactions, competitive pressures, technology changes, etc.).

• Allow people to express their fears and concerns.

• Provide mechanisms to solicit opinions and concerns, dispel rumors, and address fears.

You may need to develop multiple layers in your change strategies because people undergoing change have different needs. Change strategies for some people will center on communication. For others, the strategy may involve them in some of the team's activities and include them in key design decisions and reviews.

How do I do it?

1. **Create an organizational change plan with three components:**

   • A *change readiness assessment* that determines how ready individuals and organizations are to accept and embrace change

   • A *change path visioning* component that shows the expected path of the change process and how driving forces (accelerators) and restraining forces (resistors) will influence the expected change path

   • A *change implementation and management* component that describes the strategies to create acceptable and sustainable change in the organization

Change readiness assessment

1. **Create a critical constituencies map.**

   • This map helps you identify the extent to which the change will impact various groups in the organization.

      a) List the groups that have a stake in the change (stakeholders) in the left-hand column of a matrix.

      b) Determine the percentage of each group that will be affected by the change and record these percentages in the center column.

c) List the impact of the change (high, medium, or low) on the group in the right-hand column.

A Sample Critical Constituencies Map

Organization	Percent Affected	Change Impact
Sales	50%	High
Marketing	10%	High
Operations	75%	Low

Note: Even though the percentage of the organization affected by a change may be low, the impact on this small percentage may be high and therefore cannot be ignored.

2. Create a change readiness map.

- A change readiness map helps teams identify stakeholders' attitudes toward change. It quantifies the stakeholders' attitudes, articulates the reasons for resistance to the change, and identifies the advocates for change.

  a) List the stakeholders in the left-hand column of the matrix.

  b) Label three additional columns as "% early adopters," "% late adopters," and "% non-adopters" of the change. Label a fourth column "reasons for resistance."

  c) Determine the percentage of each group of stakeholders who will likely fit into each category and record these percentages in the appropriate cells.

  d) Identify the reasons why each group could be resistant to the change and record this information in the appropriate cells.

A Sample Change Readiness Map

Organization	% Early Adopters	% Late Adopters	% Non-Adopters	Reasons for Resistance
Sales	20	50	30	In conflict with bonus pay system
Marketing	10	10	80	Doesn't fit current product mix
Operations	50	40	10	Causes minor restructuring of department

3. Create a stakeholder commitment scale.

- This scale compares stakeholders' current level of commitment to the level of commitment you need them to have before the change can occur. Use the stakeholder commitment scale to:
  - Identify the individuals involved in or affected by a change.
  - Identify the degree of effort needed to bring the individuals to a level of commitment necessary for change to be implemented successfully.
  - Establish priorities and develop appropriate action plans for the different individuals involved.
- a) List the levels of commitment in the left-hand column of the matrix.
  - Discuss each of the levels with your team to clearly define them.
- b) List the stakeholders in the top row of the matrix.
- c) Use a circle to identify the level of commitment necessary from the stakeholders.

---

d) Use an X to identify the level of commitment currently demonstrated by the stakeholders.

e) Draw arrows from the X to the circle to show the degree of change that each stakeholder must undergo for the change to occur.

- Give those stakeholders with the greatest gap between the X and the circle the most attention in your planning efforts. Identify the factors that are creating the resistance in these groups and develop specific strategies to minimize or eliminate this resistance.

A Sample Stakeholder Commitment Scale

Level of Commitment	VP Sales	Manager	Customer
Enthusiastic support Will work hard to make it happen	○		○
Help it work Will lend appropriate support		○	
Hesitant Holds some reservations; won't volunteer			
Neutral Won't help; won't hurt			X
Reluctant Will have to be prodded		X	
Opposed Will openly act on and state opposition	X		
Hostile Will block at all costs			

Change path visioning

The change path visioning process shows change as a series of steps, with intermediate transition states occurring between the current and desired states. By understanding the transition stages and the forces that compel people to leave or stay at each stage, you can craft a workable plan for managing change.

1. Develop a visioning process.

- At each stage, ask:
  - What works here?
  - What does not work here?
  - What keeps people here?
  - What would happen if we stayed at this stage?
  - Why would people not want to be at this stage?

2. Use this information to plan movement to the next step until the desired state is reached.

A Sample Change Path Visioning Plan

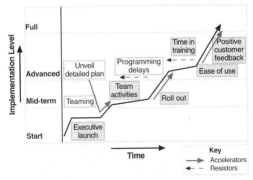

In this example, some events, such as positive customer feedback and a detailed plan, will help to speed up the implementation pace while others such as programming delays and training will take more time and slow implementation. Visualizing when and where these events are likely to occur on the change path will help the design team create a realistic vision of the change process.

Change implementation and management

Change implementation links the organization's readiness for change with the visioning process.

Communication is important in creating and managing change. Ongoing communication:

- Keeps key stakeholders informed of progress.
- Enables stakeholders to plan resource allocation.
- Assists in aligning the project with other initiatives.
- Creates buy-in and support for the design.
- Prevents misunderstandings, which can impede or stop the project.

Use a communication plan as your primary mechanism to link the visioning process to the change.

1. **When creating a communication plan, ask:**
   - Who are the stakeholders?
   - What information needs to be conveyed to them?
   - How should the information best be conveyed (e.g., by email, meeting, etc.)?
   - How often should we communicate?

Tip Refer back to your commitment scale to determine who your stakeholders are. Typical stakeholders include:

- Managers whose budgets, results, schedules, or resources will be affected by the project.
- Customers targeted by the design.
- Suppliers who will provide materials or services for the design.
- Internal departments or groups whose work flows into the new design or whose work depends on the new design.

You may need to add additional stakeholders once you select your design concept.

2. **Record your answers to the questions above and distribute this information to the stakeholders in your organization.**

1.4 Identify Risks

Design projects face a number of risks. Anticipate where the key risks of failure are and develop a plan to address those risks:

- Identify known and potential risks for the project. When chartering a team, you may not know many of the risks because you have not yet chosen the specific design. Identify any known risks in the initial charter as well as potential risks that you anticipate.
- Indicate when and how the risks will be addressed. Also indicate at which point in the design process you expect to have the data to identify the real risks in the project. Update the risk assessment as the project moves forward.

Common potential risks include inadequate customer or business information, inadequate measures for the design, a rapidly changing environment, a tendency for the project scope to extend beyond the initial project boundaries, changing resource availability, complexity, and unproven or new technologies.

The task of identifying known and potential risks and defining a plan to reduce, minimize, or eliminate these risks is referred to as mitigating risks. Use a risk management plan to mitigate the risks associated with your design project.

What is it?

A risk management plan includes a categorization of known and potential risks and a plan to address those risks.

Why use it?

To mitigate any foreseen risk associated with the design project. Failure to recognize and address a significant risk could jeopardize an entire project.

How do I do it?

1. **Brainstorm a list of all known and potential risks.**

2. **Categorize the risks by their probability of occurrence and their impact on the project.**

   • The probability of a risk impacting a project ranges from "green light" to "red light."

Assessing the Probability and Impact of Risks

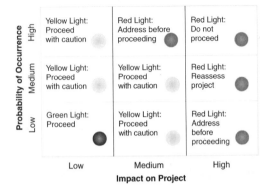

	Low	**Medium**	**High**
High	Yellow Light: Proceed with caution	Red Light: Address before proceeding	Red Light: Do not proceed
Medium	Yellow Light: Proceed with caution	Yellow Light: Proceed with caution	Red Light: Reassess project
Low	Green Light: Proceed	Yellow Light: Proceed with caution	Red Light: Address before proceeding

Probability of Occurrence

Impact on Project

3. **For each risk in the yellow or red category, determine when and how you will address the risk in the design process.**

   • Different responses are appropriate based on the perceived severity of the risk. Risks in the yellow category can be addressed further downstream in the design process, but you must address risks in the red category before proceeding further. (Not all risks in the red category result in termination of the project but some action must be taken now.) Convert all risks in the red category to yellow or green before proceeding to the next major step in the project.

A Sample Risk Management Plan

Risk Description	Category	Action
Uncertainty in market growth rate	⬤ Yellow	Collect purchase information data during VOC.
Rapid changes in technology	⬤ Yellow	Repeat technology evaluation before concept design.
Success depends on management support	⬤ Red	Launch awareness-building and organizational change.
Key project resources overcommitted	⬤ Red	Gain commitment to free resources from champion before proceeding.
Project overlaps with ongoing reengineering effort	⬤ Red	Reassess project scope and determine commonalities and differences between efforts.
No obvious customer for project	⬤ Red	Stop project.

1.5 Hold a Tollgate Review

Include regular project reviews in your project schedule to ensure that your projects are successful. There are several levels of review:

- Milestone or tollgate reviews
- Weekly reviews
- Daily reviews

In addition, design projects have three unique reviews:

- A concept review

- A high-level design review
- A detailed design review

Because design projects are often complex, resource-intensive, and linked to accomplishing key business objectives, leadership reviews at the end of each step or phase of work are critical. Reviews help maintain leadership support, and the importance of design efforts makes ongoing communication with leadership essential.

Tollgate reviews provide opportunities to:

- Establish a common understanding of the efforts to date.
- Ensure alignment and reinforce priorities.
- Provide guidance and direction.
- Demonstrate support for the project.
- Provide ongoing coaching and instruction.
- Gather data across projects on strengths and weaknesses, enabling better planning and support.
- Ensure progress.

The milestone or tollgate reviews update everyone's understanding of how the progress of the project and new information affect the business case, the business strategy to which the design is linked, the schedule, the budget, and other resourcing needs. Be sure to review key risk areas and discuss plans to eliminate or address risks. Tollgate reviews are typically held at the end of each of the Define, Measure, Analyze, Design, and Verify steps.

The sponsor and team leader may meet weekly to discuss progress, changes, surprises, resource issues, and other factors affecting the project. This weekly meeting is an opportunity for joint problem solving as it enlists the sponsor's help in addressing organizational barriers or issues.

Team leaders may also hold daily twenty-minute check-ins with team members to surface problems as early as possible, review priorities, and answer questions.

What is it?

The Tollgate Review Form is a systematic way to ensure that the tollgate at the end of each step keeps the project on track.

Why use it?

To provide consistency for design teams and help champions and sponsors review projects more efficiently and effectively.

How do I do it?

1. Review the purpose of the step and discuss how you have achieved that purpose with this project.

2. Review the checklist of deliverables to ensure that these have been completed.

3. Answer the specific questions that describe what was done in this step and what will need to be done in the next step. Use a graphical Storyboard method to present this information at the tollgate review meeting.

> **Tip** Some generic questions are listed in the sample form on the next page. Revise the questions to suit the needs of your particular organization and design project.

The Define Tollgate Review Form

Define:
Develop a clear definition of the design project

Deliverables:

- ☐ Project charter
- ☐ Project plan
- ☐ Organizational change plan
- ☐ Risk management plan
- ☐ Storyboard presentation

- What is the problem or opportunity you are trying to address?
- What is the specific process, product, or service you are (re)designing?
- What are the strategic drivers for the project?
- Why is the DMADV method right for this project?
- What is the scope of the project?
- What is the project timeline and completion date?
- Are additional team resources needed?
- What are the major risks associated with the project? How will these risks be addressed?
- How will you ensure the organization embraces and supports changes resulting from the design?
- What barriers have you encountered?
- Is your project plan on track?
- What are your key learnings from the Define step?
- What are your next steps?

©2004 GOAL/QPC

Measure
Customer Requirements

D
A
D
V

Why do it?
To translate the Voice of the Customer (VOC) into CTQs.

Tools used in this step:
- The Customer Segmentation Tree
- The Data Collection Plan
- Customer research tools:
  - Interviews
  - Contextual Inquiry
  - Focus Groups
  - Surveys
- The Voice of the Customer Table
- Affinity Diagrams
- The Kano Model
- Performance Benchmarking
- The Quality Function Deployment (QFD) Matrix
- The CTQ Risk Matrix
- The Multistage Plan
- Tollgate Review Forms

Outputs of this step:
- Prioritized CTQs
- Updated risk managment plan and multistage

project plan, if appropriate

- A tollgate review and updated Storyboard

Key questions answered in this step:

- Who are the customers of the process, product, or service?
- Who are the most important customers?
- Do all customers have the same needs? If not, how can we segment customers?
- How do we collect data on customers' needs?
- How do we understand customers' most important needs?
- What are the critical design requirements to meet the customers' needs?
- What are the performance targets that the design should meet to satisfy customers?
- What are the risks associated with not meeting all of the performance requirements immediately?
- Is a phased approach necessary to meet all of the key CTQs?

How do I do it?

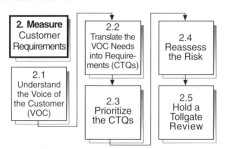

©2004 GOAL/QPC

2.1 Understand the Voice of the Customer

The term *Voice of the Customer* describes customers' needs and their perceptions of your process, product, or service. It includes all aspects of the relationship with the customer with regard to quality, cost, and delivery.

Note: The Measure step focuses on understanding customers' expressed and latent needs. However, understanding customer requirements is not limited to the work in the Measure step. Customer research occurs throughout the DMADV process. You may gather market information in the Define step to build a business case for the project. You might involve customers in the concept review at the end of the Analyze step and in the development of high-level and detailed designs in the Design step. Customers also provide feedback on prototypes and can work closely with the design sub-teams in the Design step, giving frequent, rapid feedback as the design unfolds. And you may ask customers to participate in the pilot in the Verify step; however, their activity in the pilot is simply to help with minor adjustments to the overall system (i.e., you should not be discovering important new requirements in the pilot).

Understanding the Voice of the Customer is critical. VOC data helps an organization:

- Align design and improvement efforts with the business strategy.

- Decide what processes, products, and services to offer or enhance.

- Identify the critical features and performance requirements for processes, products, and services.

- Identify the key drivers of customer satisfaction.

  Tip If you are collecting VOC data to design a new process, product, or service, remember that what customers say may not match their behavior. For example, when asked how long they are willing to wait on the phone, customers may say one minute, when in fact, they are only willing to tolerate twenty seconds when they are put on hold in a real situation.

Be sure to find out what your customers need and will tolerate instead of what their perception might be.

(For more information on uncovering customer needs, see Richard B. Chase and Sriram Dasu's article, "Want to Perfect Your Company's Service? Use Behavioral Science," in the June 2001 issue of the *Harvard Business Review*.)

To understand the Voice of the Customer, you need to:

- Identify the customers.
- Collect customer needs data.
- Analyze the needs data.

The outcome of understanding the Voice of the Customer is a list of prioritized needs.

2.1.1 Identify the customers

How do I do it?

1. **Identify potential customers whose interests and viewpoints are important and others whose perspectives can add value to the design.**

   - Include:
     - Customers who buy your products or services.
     - Customers who stopped buying your products or services.
     - Leading thinkers and other experts.
     - Technology leaders in the industry.
     - Strategic partners.
     - Stakeholders.

- Include your internal customers and stakeholders. Also include those who buy alternative products and services (i.e., customers who purchase from direct competitors as well as customers who choose quite different products or services to meet their needs. For example, if your organization produces frozen foods, alternative products and services could include purchasing fresh organic produce or eating in restaurants.)

2. **Identify potential customer segments.**

- Often there is no single Voice of the Customer. Different customers or types of customers have different needs and priorities. These different types of customers can be referred to as customer segments.

  If you suspect different groups will have different needs and that these differences will influence the design of your process, product, or service, think in terms of customer segments. Later, if data shows that customers have similar needs across some segments, you may be able to combine these segments. The design challenge will be to address multiple requirements across selected segments.

- To determine if segmentation is feasible for your market, ask:

  - Can we rank customers in order of importance?

  - Does the expected return on investment for the identified customer segments warrant a custom solution? How will this impact subsequent design phases, manufacturability, and marketing?

  - Can we easily reach the customers in each segment to collect the data we need?

  - Will the targeted customers respond to research efforts?

Tip When segmenting *business* customers, consider:

- Company demographics such as industry, size, and location.

- Operating variables such as technology used, product used, brand used, technical strength or weakness, and financial strength or weakness.

- Purchasing approach such as purchasing organization, powerful influencers, and policies.

- Situational factors such as urgency of order fulfillment, product application, and size of order.

- Personal characteristics such as buyer/seller similarity and attitudes toward risk.

When segmenting *residential* customers, consider:

- Geography.

- Demographics such as age, sex, education, and income.

- Product usage such as rate of use, end use, brand loyalty, and price sensitivity.

- Purchasing roles such as initiator, influencer, and user.

- Psychological variables such as motivation, attitudes, learning style, and personality.

(Adapted from the 1984 *Harvard Business Review* article "How to Segment Industrial Markets" by Benson P. Shapiro and Thomas V. Bonoma, Vol. 84, No. 3)

- Use a Customer Segmentation Tree to help you segment different types of customers.

Customer
Segmentation Tree

What is it?

A Customer Segmentation Tree is a breakdown of customer segments using a Tree Diagram and a nesting approach. The key to using the nesting approach is to maintain a balance between simplicity and enrichment.

Why use it?

- To define various customer segments
- To graphically display relationships between complex levels of segments

How do I do it?

1. **Define the first level of segmentation, and list this level on the left side of the Tree Diagram.**

   - The first level often defines segments with information that is easy to obtain (such as geography or demographics).

2. **Split the first level of segmentation into subsequent levels, adding more detail with each step. List each subsequent level to the right of the higher level, as a branch off of the higher level segment.**

   - The middle levels divide the first-level segments into more detailed descriptions such as operating variables or purchasing approaches. The inner levels focus on information (such as situational factors or personal characteristics) that can be the most difficult to obtain, but is often the most useful.

A Sample Customer Segmentation Tree

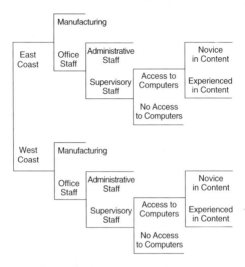

The Customer Segmentation Tree in this example shows how to deliver training to participants at multiple sites without requiring anyone to travel. Each path through the tree represents a different customer segment.

3. Prioritize the customer segments.

- Select the most important customer segments using factors such as:

  - The size of the customer segment.

  - Profit margins.

  - The frequency and volume of business transactions.

- Focus on the segment(s) whose needs align with your business strategies, including:
  - Your company's current strengths and plans.
  - New challenges and directions your company will successfully embrace.
  - Profit from serving existing customers.
  - Growth from serving new customers.

Tip Avoid immediately settling on the "classic" segmentation dimensions such as geography or demographics. These may be useful ways of segmenting existing business, but the new design may require different segments based on the charter and the strategic objectives of the project. Take an unbiased look at the segmentation options available before finalizing your choices.

2.1.2 Collect customer needs data

Customers may communicate directly with you when they have a problem, but in other instances, you may have to actively seek out information on issues that relate to customers' needs. There are two basic systems you can use to collect customer needs data and capture customer information–*reactive systems* and *proactive systems*.

Reactive systems:

- Are initiated by the customer (e.g., as complaints, returns, credits, and warranty claims).
- Provide information about a current process, product, or service.
- Can be biased because they only collect data from those customers who have a need to contact the company (usually because they are unhappy).
- Generally gather data from current and former customers on issues or problems, unmet needs, or their interest in a particular product or service.

Proactive systems:

- Are initiated by your organization rather than the customer (e.g., as market research, customer interviews, surveys, and focus groups).

- Provide information on potential new products or new uses for existing products.

- Can be less biased than reactive systems and more likely to uncover latent needs (if the systems are designed well).

- Generally gather data from selected customer groups such as current customers, former customers, noncustomers, and competitors' customers.

- Reactive systems help capture all of the ways in which customers communicate their needs. Most businesses already have daily contact with their customers in which customers share their opinions about what is important to them. Organizations generally use this contact information to solve a customer's immediate needs. But you should explore this often-underused source of information before attempting to gather new information. You can learn a lot about improving existing processes, products, and services by putting extra effort into categorizing and analyzing the data from reactive sources, and reviewing this data periodically to identify patterns, trends, and other opportunities.

- Proactive systems help capture data on unstated needs and validate your assumptions about customer needs. In proactive systems, *you* initiate the contact with customers. You design and undertake targeted customer contact to gather information specifically related to your project. Ideally, your contact will include face-to-face interviews or customer visits. To maximize efficiency, be sure to integrate your efforts with any ongoing customer contact in your organization (i.e., request that your customer service or marketing staff ask additional questions during regular contact with customers, or ask to observe customers in their workplace during a scheduled visit).

Note: An advantage to using proactive research is that it allows you to gather information on both stated and unstated needs and avoid some of the bias associated with reactive data collection methods.

How do I do it?

Tip Start your data collection process by collecting reactive data because it is generally easier to obtain and can provide a basic understanding of customer concerns (allowing you to better focus your proactive work). Follow up with information from proactive systems to better expand your understanding of customer needs and to quantify the importance that customers place on various characteristics.

1. **Collect and summarize existing data.**

   • Existing data can lead to hypotheses about customer requirements that you may decide to verify with further proactive customer research.

   • Some data may already be collected, but you may need to institute processes to locate, extract, and summarize the data.

2. **Analyze this data using the appropriate tools (e.g., Pareto Charts or Control Charts).**

   • Make a few preliminary conclusions from the relevant existing data.

3. **Determine which preliminary conclusions you need to validate with new customer research.**

   • Determine if you reached the right conclusions from the existing data.

---

4. **Consider additional broad questions to understand your customers' needs and extend your thinking beyond existing products and services.**

   • Use proactive research to determine what else you need to learn to understand customer requirements that go beyond responses to current products and services.

   Tip Use customer research to move toward greater certainty about what customers need and what priorities they put on those needs. Keep in mind that gathering and analyzing customer information costs time and money. On one side are the costs of risks from having too little information. On the other side are the costs associated with gathering more information. Find the balance point between the risk you can tolerate and the certainty you can afford.

5. **After identifying the scope of data collection, develop a plan to collect the data.**

   • Ask:

     - What are the goals for data collection?

     - What additional data do we need to gather?

     - What is the right level of detail at which to collect data?

     - How do we collect true "needs" information?

     - What methods should we use to collect the data?

     - How should we record the data?

     - What is the appropriate sample size?

     - How much piloting / preliminary analysis is needed?

     - How will we reduce sources of error and variation in the data collection?

Use a VOC Data Collection Plan form like the one on the following page to record the details of your plan.

VOC Data Collection Plan Form

PROJECT:

Who	What and Why
Customers and Segments	Indicate specifically what you want to know about your customers. Develop customized versions of the following questions that you can ask during face-to-face interviews: • What's important to you? • What's a defect? • How are we doing? How do we compare to our competitors? • What do you like? What don't you like?

Sources

Put an X next to the data sources you think will be useful for this project.

Reactive Sources
- ❏ Complaints
- ❏ Problem or service hotlines
- ❏ Technical-support calls
- ❏ Customer-service calls
- ❏ Claims, credits
- ❏ Sales reporting
- ❏ Product-return information
- ❏ Warranty claims
- ❏ Web page activity
- ❏ Other:

Proactive Sources
- ❏ Interviews
- ❏ Focus groups
- ❏ Surveys
- ❏ Comment cards
- ❏ Sales visits/calls
- ❏ Direct observation
- ❏ Market research/monitoring
- ❏ Benchmarking
- ❏ Quality scorecards
- ❏ Other:

Summary: Which, How Many, How, and When

On a separate sheet, summarize your plans to gather and use reactive and proactive sources. Indicate how much data you will get, how you will get it, and when. Include, for instance, the number of interviews or surveys you plan to conduct, which customers you will contact, when you will start and end the data-collection process, and so on.

Customers don't always express their true needs. They often mistakenly express:

- Perceived needs
- Misstatements of use
- Features and functions
- Quality characteristics or measures, or
- Targets

as real needs, making the discovery of their true needs more difficult.

To ensure that the VOC data collection focuses on true needs as much as possible, ask questions to reveal the needs that underlie what customers say. A customer who expresses a perceived need by saying "I want a taxi within ten minutes of calling for one" may really be saying "I want to reach my final destination on time." A customer who provides a product or service feature by stating "I need a performance summary report every day" may really be saying "I need a way to monitor service performance every day." And a customer who says "I'm concerned about average speed of answer" has translated his customer need into design language; he may actually be saying "I'm waiting too long on the phone."

> **Tip** When you collect VOC data, focus on the true needs as much as possible. You can then identify true needs as:
>
> - Stated needs: Needs that customers verbalize, often expressed in response to proactive data collection questions or through reactive means such as complaints.
>
> - Latent needs: Needs that customers may not verbalize, either because the customers think they are too obvious to state or because customers are themselves unaware or unable to formulate the need.

Customers often fail to verbalize latent needs for new designs so make sure that you uncover and collect latent needs data.

An exploration of needs data begins with an analysis of existing data, continues with data collection from individuals and groups of similar customers, and ends with a verification of the findings from many customers.

The Data Collection Process

When collecting VOC information:

1. Proceed from high level to detailed.

- Often, collected needs are too general (e.g., "good customer service" is not specific enough to design customer service operations). However, because data collection is expensive and time-consuming, it is useful to generate some ideas about the general areas that you need to explore before plunging into details. The needs obtained at the most detailed level will then help you generate design solutions.

2. Proceed from qualitative to quantitative.

- Focus your initial VOC effort on identifying the qualitative categories of needs and on uncovering new needs. After identifying the qualitative categories that you should gather information in, you can then quantitatively prioritize the detailed needs.

Use interviews, contextual inquiries, focus groups, and surveys as proactive tools to capture VOC data. Avoid using surveys or questionnaires until you have had in-depth discussions with individuals or focus groups because these tools don't uncover new needs; they help verify needs identified through other means. Use surveys and questionnaires to collect quantitative information on priorities and to validate your conclusions by checking with a larger group.

Interview

What is it?

An interview collects stated needs from the customer's perspective on a variety of issues regarding the process, product, or service. Information from interviews is recorded word for word from the customer's responses.

Why use it?

- To identify what is important to customers
- To uncover new and unexpected information
- To reach people who may not participate in other data-collection methods
- To confirm your design team's theories

- To add information that clarifies an issue and helps you better understand why an issue is important to customers

- To validate conclusions and themes

How do I do it?

1. **Select a cross-section of potential customers.**

   - Include customers from all key segments.

2. **Prepare for the interview.**

   - Define the objective of the interview.

   - Determine what information you need.

   - Decide specifically whom to interview.

     - Select people to interview based on the range of customer perspectives needed. The individuals selected may need to represent a key customer segment (such as an industry) as well as a function (such as sales). The individual may also need to represent the user, the "approver," or the purchaser of the product or service.

   - Set a time limit for the interview.

   - Write the interview questions and develop an interview guide.

   - Train the interviewers.

   - Schedule the interview.

   Caution: Interviewers can inadvertently introduce bias by the wording of their questions and with their verbal and nonverbal responses to answers. To reduce this bias, use experienced professional interviewers or spend sufficient time wording, testing, and revising the questions and question sequences before conducting the first interview. Interviews also have the disadvantage of a small sample size; the data analysis may require qualitative tools and can be time-consuming.

3. Conduct the interview.

- Whenever possible, have two people conduct each interview. Allow one person to focus on the questions and interaction while the other person takes verbatim notes.

- Conduct the interviews face-to-face, by phone, or by videoconference. (Phone or videoconference interviews are particularly useful when customers are geographically dispersed.)

- Be clear about the purpose of the interview. Let the interviewee do most of the talking, and listen actively. When setting up the interview, inform the interviewee of the time commitment (most interviews last 1–2 hours) and have a backup plan if time needs to be cut short.

- Open the interview by building rapport and trust. Tell the respondent he or she may ask questions at any time. Explain note-taking methods and ask permission to record answers. Address confidentiality issues and have a back-up plan if permission is not granted. Before asking the first question, solicit and address any questions or concerns.

- During the interview, be relaxed and conversational. Check your understanding and ask probing questions to ensure that answers are complete. Watch the time and pace yourself, covering all of the key points within the time limit. If you want the respondent to rate or rank items, ask at the end of the interview.

- At the end of the interview, thank respondents for their time and participation. Ask if you can be in touch in case you need any clarification. If your organization is willing, ask respondents if they would like a summary of the findings.

4. **After the interview, summarize your learnings while the interview is fresh in your mind and record any ideas that could enhance future interviews.**

Contextual Inquiry

What is it?

Contextual inquiry is a data-gathering method using a master/apprentice model rather than an interviewer/subject model to collect latent needs about a process, product, or service.

The attitude of apprenticeship is one of curiosity and learning. The person doing the work is an expert at his or her work and the apprentice pays attention to the details in an open, nonjudgmental way and asks exploring questions. The questions help the person doing the work reflect on the work; the reflection helps the questioner understand the work.

Why use it?

- To uncover the unstated details of a work process
- To discover new uses and features for processes, products, and services
- To explore actual vs. intended uses
- To identify latent as well as stated needs

How do I do it?

1. **Visit a customer's workplace to observe work as it happens.**

2. **Collaborate with the customer in understanding his or her work.**
   - Be sure to maintain your perspective as the apprentice throughout the inquiry.

3. **Interpret the findings from your observations.**
   - If possible, combine the perspectives from multiple contextual interviews to produce an overall picture.

   Tip The questions for a contextual inquiry grow out of the observations of the work. Do not develop a rigorous interview guide for a contextual inquiry.

   Caution: Contextual inquiry is not as useful if the design is not connected to a current process, product, or service. It also has the disadvantage of a small sample size.

What is it?

A focus group is a planned and facilitated discussion that records interaction among participants and reveals factors that influence participants' attitudes, feelings, and behavior.

Why use it?

- To define and understand the requirements of each customer segment

- To understand the priorities of each customer segment

- To generate synergy among participants with common interests (which stimulates new ideas)

- To allow open-ended comments and provide insight into opinions, attitudes, and opinion shifts

- To provide insight into complex behaviors or motivations

- To deepen your understanding of participants' thought processes

How do I do it?

1. Plan the focus group session.

- Determine why you are holding the focus group.

- Determine the criteria for whom to involve in the focus group. (Focus groups usually include 7–13 people.) Identify which customer segment each focus group will represent and choose an experienced moderator(s) to help you plan and conduct the sessions.

- Decide on a structure and flow for the discussion. (Most focus groups sessions consist of in-depth discussion on a limited number of topics.)

- Determine the location and schedule. (Sessions usually last 2–4 hours.)

- Determine what resources you will need for a successful session.

- Limit the number of questions.

Tip Conduct at least three focus groups to ensure that the data is representative. If the customer segments have different needs, complete at least one focus group with each segment to verify

---

that they do have different needs and to understand how their needs differ. Continue conducting focus groups until you fail to learn anything new.

2. Conduct the focus group session.

- Introduce the purpose, participants, topic, and expectations of the session.
- Set the ground rules for discussion.
- Facilitate the discussion.

3. Summarize and analyze your findings.

Like interview questions, focus group questions should be predetermined, open-ended, logically sequenced, nonthreatening, clear, and simple. In addition, focus group questions should move from broad topics to specific ones.

> **Caution:** Focus groups are often difficult to facilitate and manage. Typically, the interviewer has less control over the interaction than in individual interviews, the data analysis requires skills in qualitative interactive research, and the logistics can be very challenging. Be prepared to provide an experienced moderator to ensure a successful outcome. It may be helpful to use a moderator who is not directly involved in or affected by the project.

Surveys

What is it?

A survey is a structured data collection method that helps to verify the conclusions identified using previous methods.

Why use it?

- To efficiently collect and quantify information from a large population
- To verify and prioritize needs identified by other data collection methods
- To easily quantify data
- To provide anonymity

Interviews, observations, and focus groups identify needs. Surveys follow these tools and verify that the needs are, in fact, characteristic of the whole segment that the participants represent.

> **Caution:** Surveys have several disadvantages including high expense and a low response rate. Be careful in your use of them.

How do I do it?

1. **Determine the objectives and appropriate type(s) of survey (i.e., mail, phone, electronic, individual, or group).**

2. **Determine the sample size.**

   - Sampling involves collecting data from a portion of the population and using that portion to draw conclusions or make inferences about the entire population. Sampling may be necessary because collecting data from everyone in the population may be too expensive or too time-consuming. When designed well, a relatively small amount of data can often provide very sound conclusions.

   > **Tip** Use the following four factors to determine how many samples are needed:

   1. What type of data (discrete or continuous) you will collect

   2. What you want to do (e.g., describe a char-

acteristic [such as the mean or proportion] for a whole group with a certain precision [+/- "x" units], or compare group characteristics [i.e., find differences between group means or group proportions] at a specific power [i.e., the probability you will use to detect a certain difference])

3. What you think the standard deviation will be

4. How confident you want to be (usually 95%)

Tip Because sampling can be complex, enlist the help of a statistician in determining sample size.

3. **Identify the information you need to collect.**

4. **Write the survey questions and develop measurement scales.**

   • Prevent response bias by avoiding:

     - Loaded questions: Value-laden language that is likely to bias the response (e.g., "Do you support ridiculous Proposition X?").

     - Questions that lead respondents toward a particular answer (e.g., "Isn't it true that men are more likely to speed than women?").

     - Ambiguity: Questions that are not focused enough to obtain the information you need (e.g., "How often do you buy fast food?" vs. "In the last ten times you've eaten out for lunch, how often have you purchased each of the following types of food. . .?").

     - Too much or too little specificity.

     - More than one topic or issue per question.

   • Ensure that participants can answer all questions meaningfully by using specific options or scales (i.e., use a limited number of open-ended questions).

Tip An interval scale is the most common type of measurement scale used in surveys. An interval scale is a continuum with equal intervals marked off and often includes an odd number of points to provide a neutral midpoint. Place the options on the scale in order (e.g., low = 1 and high = 5) and ensure that the difference from one option to the next is consistent across the scale. Use interval scales to measure the level of:

- Agreement (strongly disagree to strongly agree).
- Satisfaction (extremely dissatisfied to extremely satisfied).
- Importance (extremely unimportant to extremely important).

5. Specify the requirements for coding.

- Be clear about how you will handle the survey responses so that the survey's design will give you the information that you are seeking.
- Define, up front, how you will "code" the survey answers after the surveys are completed and returned (e.g., to code responses about customer segments, you might label the parts of the survey that deal with customer segments).

6. Create the survey.

7. Test, pilot, and finalize the survey.

2.1.3 Analyze the needs data

How do I do it?

1. **Check the VOC statements collected in the previous step.**

    • Review the language data to remove duplicates.

    • Reword the data as necessary to reflect consistent phrasing in the customer's voice (e.g., translate all negatives into positive statements).

2. **Separate the needs from solutions, targets, and measurements.**

    Tip Save any functions or solutions until later when you develop concepts. Consider them at that point, along with the other solutions you will develop. Save targets and measurements until you translate the customer needs into requirements. Consider the measurements along with the other measures generated by your team; consider the targets during the target-setting process.

    • Use a VOC Table to assist in sorting needs from other types of comments.

What is it?

A Voice of the Customer Table helps sort needs from solutions, targets, measurements, and other types of comments.

©2004 GOAL/QPC

Why use it?
- To structure a sorting process involving large quantities of data
- To help explain the sorting process to others

How do I do it?
1. Construct a table by listing the categories (e.g., solutions, targets, measurements, and needs) across the top row of the table and listing customer verbatims in the left column.
2. Identify what category each verbatim applies to. Place an X in the corresponding cell.
3. For each verbatim that is not a need, spend a few moments with your team to translate the customer statement into the need underlying the statement. Add that need to the table and continue on with the next verbatim.

A Sample VOC Table

Customer Statement	Solution	Measure	Target	Need
Need agent to call after order is received	X			
Need order fulfilled in 24 hours			X	
Need high order-fulfillment rate		X		
Need stock replenished before it runs out				X

3. **Organize the needs.**

   • Select the needs from the VOC Table and sort them into common levels of detail using an Affinity Diagram.

Affinity Diagram

What is it?

An Affinity Diagram organizes large amounts of language data (ideas, opinions, issues, etc.) into groupings based on the natural relationships between the items.

Why use it?

   • To organize and summarize natural groupings among a large number of ideas

   • To categorize the customer verbatims of the VOC

How do I do it?

1. **Sort through all of the information you have collected (from interviews, focus groups, surveys, etc.) and select those comments that reflect needs related to the design project.**

2. **Write these needs on cards or Post-it® Notes.**

   • Keep the need statements used in the Affinity Diagram in the customer's own language if at all possible. Avoid using single words; use, at minimum, a verb and a noun.

   Tip In general, the more specific and concrete the statement, the more valuable it will be. For ex-

---

©2004 GOAL/QPC

ample, a vague statement such as "I want good service" provides no clue about what you can do to make that customer happier. Specific statements that relate to a particular requirement, such as "I want my questions to be answered correctly the first time," provide much more information about that customer's needs and expectations.

Note: For more detail on selecting and sorting customer statements, see *Voices into Choices: Acting on the Voice of the Customer* by Gary Burchill and Christina Hepner Brodie, Oriel Inc., Madison, WI.

Tip A "typical" Affinity Diagram has 40–60 items; it is not unusual to have 100–200 ideas.

3. **Have team members simultaneously sort the ideas (without talking) into 5–10 related groupings.**

• Have team members move each Post-it® Note where it best fits for them. Tell them not to ask before moving a Post-it® Note; simply move any note that belongs in another group.

Note: Sorting will slow down or stop when each person feels sufficiently comfortable with the groupings.

Tip Sort in silence to focus on the meaning behind and connections among all ideas, instead of the emotions and "history" that often arise in discussions.

Tip As an idea is moved back and forth, have team members try to see the logical connection that the other person is making. If this movement continues beyond a reasonable point, have them agree to create a duplicate Post-it® Note.

Tip It is okay for some notes to stand alone. These "loners" can be as important as others that fit into groupings naturally.

4. **Use consensus to create summary or header cards for each grouping.**

a) Gain a quick consensus on a phrase that captures the central idea / theme of each grouping; record it on a Post-it® Note and place it at the top of each grouping as a *draft* header card.

b) For each grouping, agree on a concise sentence that combines the grouping's central idea and what all of the specific Post-it® Notes add to that idea; record it and replace the draft card with this *final* header card.

Tip Spend the extra time you need to create good header cards. Strive to capture the essence of *all* of the ideas in each grouping. Shortcuts here can greatly reduce the effectiveness of the final Affinity Diagram.

Tip It is possible that a note within a grouping could become a header card. However, don't choose the "closest one" because it's convenient. The hard work of creating new header cards often leads to breakthrough ideas.

c) Divide large groupings into subgroups as needed and create appropriate subheads.

d) Draw the final Affinity Diagram connecting all finalized header cards with their groupings.

In the example on the next page, data collected on the "billing process" is analyzed using an Affinity Diagram.

A Sample Affinity Diagram

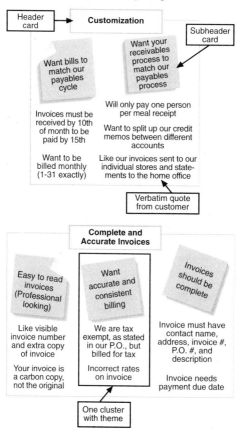

4. Check the needs list for completeness.

- Use the Kano Model to ensure that you have not omitted any critical needs.

Kano Model

What is it?

The Kano Model helps to describe which needs, if fulfilled, contribute to customer dissatisfaction, neutrality, or delight. It identifies the:

- "Must Be" needs: Those needs that the customer expects (e.g., airline safety). If Must Be needs are unfulfilled, the customer is dissatisfied; however, even if they are completely fulfilled, the customer is not particularly satisfied.

- "More Is Better" needs: Those needs that have a linear effect on customer satisfaction (e.g., faster airport check-ins). The more these needs are met, the more satisfied customers are.

- "Delighter" needs: Those needs that do not cause dissatisfaction when not present but satisfy the customer when they are (e.g., serving hot chocolate chip cookies during an airline flight).

Why use it?

To identify and prioritize the full range of customers' needs.

How do I do it?

1. Gather sorted customer needs from an Affinity Diagram.

---

2. **Review the themes from the Affinity Diagram and sort them into the three categories in the Kano Model (Must Be, More Is Better, and Delighters).**

3. **If there are very few or no needs listed in one of the categories, collect additional customer data.**

    Tip Customers generally cannot express what their basic expectations are or what would delight them. Therefore, when you prioritize customer needs based on what they say is important, remember that customers generally identify only More Is Better characteristics. Use other means (such as direct observation of customer use) to identify and set priorities for Must Be needs and Delighters.

4. **After you have collected additional data, return to the Kano categories and complete the sorting of customer needs.**

5. **Prioritize the customer needs you will use when you develop the CTQs.**

    Tip Include all Must Be needs because, if absent, they will create customer dissatisfaction. Consider the importance of More Is Better needs to provide steady and strong increases in satisfaction. Include a few Delighters that will increase satisfaction dramatically. Also consider how these categories relate to your company's competitive advantage.

Customer Expectations for a Hotel Room

	Must Be	**More Is Better**	**Delighters**
Hotel Room	• Bed • Clean towels • Phone • Coffee maker	• Number/ thickness of towels • Size of room	• Fruit basket upon arrival • Balcony • Free movies

Tip Customer needs change over time. A Delighter today might be a Must Be need tomorrow. Different customer segments might also have different needs. For example, a business traveler might consider an iron in a hotel room a Must Be need but the size of the desk's work surface a More Is Better need. However, a family traveling on vacation might consider free movies and video games a More Is Better need and consider the desk size irrelevant.

Tip Double-check your work to ensure that you have not inadvertently missed a Must Be need. And because you gain competitive advantage through Delighters, identify additional Delighters if they are few in number.

5. **Establish priorities for the detailed needs.**

   • There are two possible types of prioritization– *qualitative prioritization* and *quantitative prioritization*.

   • Qualitative prioritization uses low/medium/high scales, extracts priorities from the frequency of being mentioned, and uses the Must Be, More Is Better, and Delighter Kano Model classifications.

   • Quantitative prioritization uses rating or ranking scales like the ones listed below.

Quantitative Prioritization Scales

Scale	Description
Absolute importance	Rate on a scale of 1 (least important) to 5 (most important)
Relative importance	Assign 100 points between needs; determine the relative importance through a series of pairwise comparisons (e.g., A is more important than B).
Ordinal importance	Rank-order from most to least important

©2004 GOAL/QPC

Tip Because quantitative prioritization uses customer ratings and rankings to prioritize needs, it
is the recommended approach to capture and
understand the Voice of the Customer.

2.2 Translate the VOC Needs into Require-
ments (CTQs)

In most situations, customers express their needs in everyday
language. But the design team needs to express the
requirements to design a process, product, or service in precise technical terms. Therefore, you must use a translation
process to convert the needs of the customers into the language
of the design team. These translated requirements, expressed in business or engineering language, are the CTQs.

Note: In some cases, the translation from needs to measures
is obvious so this substep may be unnecessary. For example,
the need "quick response" can be directly translated into
the measure "speed of response." But for less tangible needs
(such as "I want to feel welcome when I walk into your
business"), thinking first about characteristics of the need
(e.g., feeling welcome includes politeness, friendliness,
etc.) will help in identifying measures to meet these needs.

Remember that each CTQ should have:

- A quality characteristic that specifies how the
  designed process, product, or service will meet
  the customer need.

- A quantitative measure for the performance of
  the quality characteristic.

  (**Note:** Remember to create clear operational
  definitions of the measures for the CTQs.)

- A target value that represents the desired level of
  performance that the characteristic should meet.

- Specification limits that define the performance
  limits that customers will tolerate.

Necessary Components
for Two Sample CTQs

CTQ	Customer Need	Quality Characteristic	Measure	Target	Specification Limits
Designing a pizza delivery service	"I want my pizza to be hot when I get it."	Hotness of pizza	Temperature (in °F)	125°F	Lower limit = 120°F; Upper limit = 130°F
Customer service	"I want the right answer from the first person I speak with on the phone."	Phone transfers	Number of transfers before the customer receives an answer	Zero transfers	98%

To translate the VOC needs into requirements (CTQs), you need to:

- Generate the CTQs.
- Set targets and specifications.

2.2.1 Generate the CTQs

To generate CTQs for each of the prioritized needs from substep 2.1:

1. **Select the appropriate level of need to focus on.**

    Tip Typically, teams use lower level needs to generate measures. If there are 30–60 needs at this lower level, the task of generating measures can be quite daunting. To make this task easier, you should ini-

---

tially develop characteristics for the first- or second-level needs and use the QFD Matrix (explained in greater detail later in this chapter) to identify the most important characteristics. You can then generate measures using the third-level needs for only the most important characteristics.

2. **For each need at the selected level, brainstorm 1–3 quality characteristics that could address that need.**

3. **Develop measures to quantify the characteristics.**

    Tip There is no magic formula for generating measures; they are based on the knowledge of your team, the data obtained from the VOC study, and discussions between team members. Often the first few measures take a long time to generate; the task becomes easier as you get a feel for the process.

In general, the more detailed the level of analysis, the more useful and relevant the measures.

2.2.2 Set targets and specifications

1. **Set targets and specifications either:**

    • Qualitatively, using the importance of the CTQs (as expressed by the customer), competitor performance information, and internal capabilities data.

    • Quantitatively, using mathematical models of the relationship between customer satisfaction and performance.

    Caution: Determining targets and specification limits is not always easy. Target setting is both an art and a science. Targets are often set arbitrarily because organizations lack information on benchmarks and satisfaction/performance relationships (which ultimately impacts the quality of the design). Even if you cannot use formal mathematical methods, some thought and analysis is critical to setting good targets.

2. **If you have limited resources, set the highest performance targets for those measures that have the potential of providing the highest rewards.**

• Set targets to exceed competitor benchmarks for the most important CTQs but balance this expectation against the costs of meeting a high performance target and against the internal capabilities of the organization. If the organization is not capable of performing at a high level without a significant cost investment, then the returns may not justify the costs.

In the following example, higher performance targets are more critical for CTQ 1 than for CTQ 2.

Satisfaction/Performance Functions

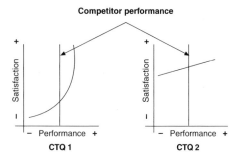

For CTQ 1, the curve between satisfaction and peformance is steep so making an investment to set a higher performance target than the competition will produce greater rewards. But failing to at least meet the competition's level of performance will result in a significant decrease in satisfaction.

For CTQ 2, the risk/reward situation is not so dire. The relationship between performance and satisfaction is shallower. As a result, a "low investment" solution of setting the performance target at or even below the competition's performance will not result in a large impact on satisfaction.

Use Performance Benchmarking to compare your organization's performance to the performance of others.

What is it?

Performance Benchmarking examines the processes, products, and services of market leaders to see how well they perform, and compares your performance capabilities against the benchmark. It is another source of information to help you define measures and set specifications.

There are nine generic categories of Performance Benchmarking:

- Customer service performance
- Product/service performance
- Core business process performance
- Support process and services performance
- Employee performance
- Supplier performance
- Technology performance
- New product/service development and innovation performance
- Cost performance

Benchmarking is usually an ongoing activity for organizations and is often part of competitive analyses

---

or strategic-planning initiatives. Benchmarking often occurs concurrently with VOC work. VOC and benchmarking data are summarized in a QFD Matrix, which is used to prioritize measures.

Why use it?

- To identify ways to measure customer requirements
- To identify best-in-class measures and specifications that help determine performance targets
- To compare your performance to the performance of other companies

How do I do it?

1. **Review any information in your organization's database that could relate to performance.**
   - This information is often a good starting point for Performance Benchmarking.

2. **Examine other sources of information such as published studies, reports, and articles.**
   - Trade journals often describe companies that excel in particular areas. Conference proceedings or reports from awards ceremonies such as the Malcolm Baldrige National Quality Award are also good sources for information on companies noted for their best practices.
   - Benchmarking databases are also a good source of performance information.

3. **Analyze your research and incorporate your findings.**
   - Based on your research, you might:
     - Identify potential measures for customer needs.
     - Identify benchmark values to consider when setting targets for CTQ measures.

- Identify how customers rank your organization's performance in relation to your competitors' performance on key measures.

2.3 Prioritize the CTQs

After completing substeps 2.1 and 2.2, you now have:

- A list of the most important customer segments.

- First-, second- and third-level needs, expressed in the customers' voice.

- A priority of needs at the appropriate level.

- Quality characteristics and measures related to these needs (i.e., the Voice of the Customer translated into design language).

- Targets and specification limits for the measures.

Now use the QFD Matrix to summarize the Voice of the Customer and your benchmarking information. The output of this tool will be the prioritized CTQs and will include measures, targets, and specifications.

What is it?

The QFD Matrix (also called the House of Quality) is a tool for summarizing the research data you gathered. The QFD Matrix uses customer needs and priorities, and summarizes any benchmarking work to allow you to understand key competitive measures and the relative performance of those measures among your competitors. Most of the work in developing a QFD Matrix involves compiling information. The information is then organized into various "rooms" that make up the matrix.

Why use it?

• To coordinate a vast amount of information and select the key measures that you will use in the rest of the design process

How do I do it?

To build a QFD Matrix:

1. **List the detailed VOC needs in the rows of the QFD Matrix and the measures for the CTQs in the matrix columns.**

2. **Fill in the cells of the matrix by asking, "If we design the process, product, or service to perform to the target specified for the measure, to what extent would we have met the need?"**

   • Use values of 1 for low correlation, 3 for medium correlation, and 9 for high correlation.

   Note: It is not necessary to fill all of the cells with a 1, 3, or 9; typically about one-third of the cells are filled.

   • An empty row indicates that a measure does not exist for the need; if the need is important, then you must define a measure for the need.

   • An empty column may indicate that the measure is not needed because it does not correspond to any need; it may also signal that a need was missed in the VOC. (Remember that customers often fail to mention Must Be needs.)

3. **Calculate the importance of each CTQ by matrix multiplication.**

   Note: Matrix multiplication is described in Room 4 of "The Rooms of the QFD Matrix" section.

   Tip If your VOC research indicates that you have customer segments with very different needs,

---

100 Measure   ©2004 GOAL/QPC

create a QFD Matrix for each segment. (Note: You may need to create different products or services for these segments.)

The importance rating calculated in step 3 is the output of the QFD exercise. Your objective in using the QFD Matrix is to find the smallest number of CTQs that meet the largest number of needs.

The Rooms of the QFD Matrix:

The QFD Matrix is divided into seven rooms.

(V) = Comes from VOC information
(B) = Comes from benchmarking information
(I) = Comes from internal expertise

Just like the rooms in a house, there are connections and relationships among the rooms.

Room	Contents	Where does this information come from?
1. Customer needs	Prioritized customer needs	The Voice of the Customer
2. Competitive comparison	Customer rating of key competitors' performance	The Voice of the Customer
3. Measures	Customer requirement measures (CTQs)	Benchmarking and the design team
4. Relationships	Relationship of CTQs to customer needs	Internal expertise and the design team
5. Technical evaluation	Actual performance of competitors on measures	Benchmarking
6. Targets	Performance required to meet CTQs/needs	Benchmarking and internal expertise
7. Correlation	Correlation between the measures	Benchmarking and internal expertise

Room 1 lists the key detailed customer needs identified by VOC research. These needs have been defined and prioritized by customers and are listed in the matrix in the customers' language.

Tip Be sure to include all Must Be needs and key More is Better needs (from the Kano analysis) in the matrix. Also include Delighters if possible.

Room 2 graphically shows how customers perceive your organization's performance and at least two competitors' performance with regard to meeting the customer needs listed in Room 1. Information gathered from VOC research is used to establish how customers perceive the performance of your organization compared to market leaders.

> **Tip** Use direct competitors who are market leaders or "excellence organizations" in your comparison. Select symbols to designate your organization's performance and the performance of the competitors you are comparing yourself with. Connect the symbols with lines to provide a better visual representation of customers' perceptions of the performance comparisons. Use a scale of 1 to 4 (with 4 representing how the "perfect" service or product performs) to rate performance.

You can easily collect the information for this room as you gather your VOC data. Use several sources of information to identify customers' perceptions of your competitors, including:

- Customer satisfaction surveys that collect information on customer ratings of both your organization and key competitors.
- Industry databases.
- Your own VOC research.

Room 3 represents the voice of your design team and lists the measures developed at the end of the VOC analysis. Ideas for measures can come from:

- The design team's work translating customer needs into CTQs (which include measures).
- Benchmarking information on how similar characteristics are measured.
- Measures currently in use for similar designs.

Note: Don't worry about having too many measures. There are often more measures than customer needs. (Each need could be addressed by multiple measures.) The QFD Matrix will help you eliminate unnecessary measures so that only the most important measures will be carried over into the next phase of the design process.

Note that some measures are intentionally vague. For example, the measure "percent information about completed order status accessible by customer" will be different depending on the design you choose and on the technology you use. (The particular technology is irrelevant; any solution should be able to meet the target specified for this measure.)

> **Tip** Make sure the measures are measurable *during* design. For example, the measure "number of complaints" won't help you during design because it can only be measured after the product or service is in the market.

> Indicate a preferred direction for the measures with arrows on the matrix (e.g., higher is better). To determine direction, ask:

> • If we increase this measurement, will that help to achieve the customer need?

> • If we reduce this measurement, will that help to achieve the customer need?

> • If we hit the measurement target, will that help to achieve the customer need?

Allow adjustments of the measure's value as you make design decisions. Do not make the measure solution-dependent to prevent biasing yourself toward one outcome.

Room 4 summarizes your thinking about the relationship between potential measures and the customers' needs.

To determine these relationships, compare each measure (from Room 3) with each need (from Room 1) and ask, "If the design meets the target set for this measure, to what extent will we meet the customer need?" Use your experience, knowledge, and expertise to help you formulate these answers.

When recording the relationships in Room 4, document the assumptions that lead to your decisions about the relationships. You can return to this documentation later when you test parts of the design.

> ***Tip*** Use symbols or numbers (9, 3, or 1) in Room 4 to show the strength of the relationship between the measures and the needs. Use a double circle (or a 9) to show a strong relationship (a direct cause-and-effect). Use a single circle (or a 3) to indicate a moderate relationship. Use a triangle (or a 1) to signal a weak relationship. Indicate that no relationship exists by leaving the space where the need and measure intersect blank.

Calculate the importance of each measure by multiplying the relationship weight (9, 3, or 1) by the importance that customers assigned to the need from the column marked "Importance" in the matrix. (Remember that customers provided these importance ratings when they prioritized or ranked their needs.) Then add the scores within the column and record the scores in the "How important" row at the bottom of the matrix. Use these scores in your discussion to check your thinking and to help identify the key measures that drive overall customer satisfaction. These key measures become the most important criteria against which to evaluate the design.

> **Caution:** Do not let the results of the calculations by themselves make the decision on prioritizing the measures. You could have a measure with a relatively low total number because it correlates with only one need. However, if that need is a Must Be need, the measure is important to keep.

Room 5 summarizes the technical benchmarking data that compares your company to your competitors with respect to performance on key measures/design requirements. Again, use symbols to represent your organization and your competitors, just as you did in Room 2. Connect the symbols using lines and rate the comparison on a scale of 1 to 5 (with 5 representing "better" in this room).

Benchmarking your own processes, products, or services and the processes, products, or services of others against key design measures that you have identified will help you to define the current level of performance. It also helps you to answer the questions:

- Have you defined the right measures to predict customer satisfaction?

- Does the process, product, or service have a perception problem (i.e., a difference in Room 2), as opposed to a technical problem (a difference in Room 5)?

Room 6 summarizes the targets established for the measures / CTQs.

You already set the target values for the design requirements in step 2.2.2. Now summarize the targets in Room 6 by examining the data gathered throughout the process and determine what you are going to do with respect to this process, product, or service.

Room 7 (the "roof") summarizes the relationships between the measures. Determine if a positive or negative relationship between measures exists by asking, "If we design to meet CTQ 1, to what extent do we satisfy or what will the effect be on CTQ 2?" If CTQ 2 will also move toward its target, then there is a positive effect. If CTQ 2 is not affected, then the effect is neutral. If CTQ 2 moves away from its target, then the effect is negative.

Use symbols (such as + and -) to represent the relationships and then evaluate the outcome. Positive relationships indicate synergy and negative relationships may indicate conflicts.

> **Tip** The design task becomes easier if you have a lot of positives in the roof of the matrix. A positive relationship indicates that if one aspect of the design is improved, other aspects will be improved as well. If you have a lot of negatives in the roof of the matrix, then you have design contentions; improving one aspect of the design may lead to problems in other aspects. If you have too many design contentions, you may have to develop more creative designs that transcend the contentions, or carefully evaluate trade-off decisions that you may have to make.

A Sample QFD Matrix

Customer needs	Percent of customer-desired technologies supported	Numbers of hours help facility is available	Number of process steps	Percent of information about completed order status accessible by customer	Percent of historical information not requiring reentry	Number of hours access is available	Importance	Competition comparison
I need to place orders when I want	3	3				9	4.3	
I need to place orders from any location	3						3.9	
I need to be able to place orders using different technologies	9						4.8	
I want an easily understandable process			3		3		4.9	
I don't want to go through many steps			9		9		4.7	
I want to know immediately if an order is confirmed				9			4.2	
I need to be able to get help if I have questions		9		3		3	4.0	
How important	68	49	57	50	57	51		
Target	100	24	4	75	90	24		
Technical evaluation							5 4 3 2 1	

Key
- ◆ Us
- ○ Competitor A
- □ Competitor B

Competition comparison: 1 2 3 4

Analyzing QFD

Use QFD analysis in the Measure step to help you see all of the information that you have gathered at once and to guide a systematic discussion of the measures as you prioritize the design requirements of the CTQs. If the design has only a few measures, you may not need to use the QFD Matrix because you may not need to prioritize the measures. However, if you have a lot of measures, you need to select a few important ones to use in the next design step as you assess potential concepts.

Use QFD analysis to also help you recognize opportunities to leverage design efforts and identify any trade-offs.

Ultimately, the QFD Matrix should serve as a validation for your business instincts. The QFD Matrix scores are simply the inputs to discussions. Your team's expertise and knowledge of the customer needs will guide your decisions.

If the QFD exercise produces results that do not match your intuition, ask the following questions before accepting the results:

- *Are all of the needs at the same level?* If needs are at various levels of detail, there may be multiple statements describing the lower level needs and a single statement describing the higher level need. This will cause the CTQs describing the lower level needs to appear to be more important than those describing the higher level need.

- *Are there multiple measurements when one might suffice?* Multiple measures correlated with the same need may result in a narrow set of design specifications concentrating on just one aspect of the design.

- *Are there any empty rows?* Empty rows indicate that the measure set is not complete.

- *Are there any empty columns?* Empty columns indicate redundant measurements or a Must Be need that is not represented in the matrix.

- *Is the matrix in Room 4 diagonal?* A diagonal pattern indicates that you may have defined the measures too narrowly.

- *Is there a mismatch between the customer evaluation data in Room 2 and the technical benchmarks in Room 5?* A discrepancy may indicate a mismatch between perception and reality.

Tip In some cases, the information from one QFD Matrix may be sufficient to proceed with the preliminary design. In other instances, you can use QFD analysis to further deploy the customer needs into design specifications via additional QFD Matrices. This is particularly true for products that are assembled from parts.

To begin a second QFD Matrix, place the measures from Room 3 of the first Matrix as the "whats" in Room 1 in the second Matrix. Then use your judgment to determine "how" to accomplish the measures. Identify the functions needed in the design and put them in Room 3 of the second QFD Matrix. Then use the same process you used previously to complete the matrix.

As shown on the following page, you can develop several matrices to achieve a very detailed understanding of the variables to control to ensure that you satisfy the customer needs.

Additional QFD Matrices
to Deploy Further Needs

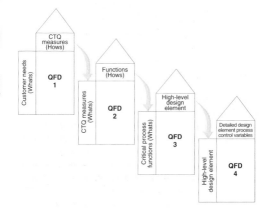

In the Measure step, the work with the QFD Matrix ends with the selection of key measures for the design and an understanding of the relationships between those measures. Now revisit your Charter and, based on current knowledge, reassess the project's scope and risks.

2.4 Reassess the Risk

After prioritizing the CTQs, reassess the risks associated with the project by asking:

- How difficult will it be to meet all of the target values of the most important CTQs?

- Do we need to adopt a phased approach to meet the target?

- What are the risks associated with not meeting the CTQs now?

- What are the risks associated with dropping some of the less important CTQs from consideration?

How do I do it?

1. **List the CTQs dropped from consideration (through your use of the QFD Matrix) and describe the associated risks.**

   - Ensure that the risks are acceptable and justify dropping the CTQs.

2. **List the CTQs whose target performance values you cannot meet now and describe the associated risks.**

3. **Determine whether you can meet the risks identified above by adopting a phased strategy.**

   - If you cannot meet all of the critical performance requirements immediately, consider a phased approach in which you create a base product or service along with a platform on which to build further enhancements.

   Caution: While an opportunity to delight customers through high-quality enhancements is possible in a phased approach, there is also a risk of dissatisfying customers who are left waiting for an enhancement.

Use the CTQ Risk Matrix and/or the Multistage Plan to support risk analysis.

What is it?

The CTQ Risk Matrix shows the risk associated with not meeting the target performance requirements and/or with dropping some of the CTQs. The CTQ Risk Matrix should consider risk along three dimensions:

1. **Inclusion: Will we include the CTQ further in the design process?**

2. **Complexity: Are the technology requirements too complex to develop all at once?**

3. **Reach: Will we meet the CTQ requirements for all customer segments simultaneously?**

Each of these dimensions involves risk and may result in customer dissatisfaction. Even if you can design the service to meet the CTQs, it may not be technically feasible to meet all of the requirements immediately. Similarly, it may not be possible to deliver the service to all market segments at the same time.

Why use it?

To identify and plan for risks

How do I do it?

1. **List the CTQ measures in the left-hand column of a matrix.**

2. **Determine if there is a design specification for the measure and list this information as a "Yes" or "No."**

---

3. List the target performance value for each CTQ.

4. Qualitatively estimate the gap between the desired target levels and the current best-in-class benchmark or target needed, based on VOC data. List this information as "the ability to meet the target with the base platform."

   • The first design phase or base platform represents the first version of the design that you will implement.

   • If the gap is very large, it may not be possible to close the gap in the first design implementation.

5. List an estimate of the risk associated with not meeting the target.

6. Describe the risk mitigation plan for each CTQ.

7. Develop a phased approach if you cannot meet all included CTQs immediately.

   • Each phase is a sequential time period for implementing the design. Describe the design phases using a Multistage Plan.

A Sample CTQ Risk Matrix

CTQ measure	Design specification	Target performance value	Ability to meet target with base platform	Associated risk	Risk mitigation plan
Percent of customer-desired technologies supported	Yes	100%	Medium	High–significant impact on customer satisfaction	Accelerate ability to support all technologies
Percent of historical information not requiring reentry of data	Yes	75%	Low	High–key contributor to customer satisfaction	Include in extension platform
Number of hours online help facility is available	No	N/A	N/A	Low–met by overall accessibility requirement	None
Percent of information about historical orders accessible	No	60%	Depends on other CTQs	Medium–may not be completely met by other CTQs	Revisit after concept selection is complete

Multistage
Plan

What is it?

The Multistage Plan specifies the phases you will use to implement the process, product, or service design. The cells of the Multistage Plan matrix describe the features of the design in each time period and for each customer segment. The multiple phases of the design are often indicated by color-coding.

Why use it?

- To create phased plans to deal with risk
- To keep the scope of the project contained so that it is manageable
- To ensure that the first generation of a design will get to the market within the specified time window
- To provide a market presence for the organization while implementing the later stages of a design
- To learn from customer reaction to the first phase of the design while implementing the later phases of the design

How do I do it?

1. Create a matrix with the names of the design phases in the left-hand column of the matrix and the customer market segments for the design along the top row of the matrix.
2. Fill in the cells of the matrix with the features of the design that could apply to each market segment in the specified phase.

- The complexity of the implemented design may vary for each phase and customer segment. Use the following definitions to describe the design complexity:

  - The *Base Platform* is the base design. Typically the least complex design, it may not meet the performance targets for some CTQs.

  - The *Platform Extensions* are the more-complex extensions to the base design.

  - A *New Platform* is a completely different design, which is often out-of-scope for the current project.

  Note that the base platform and its extensions reflect differences in the complexity of the design. It is not necessary for every customer segment to have a base platform implemented first, followed by the platform extensions; for some critical segments, you may need to implement a design that includes the platform extensions in the first phase to maintain a competitive advantage.

  Tip Keep the feature descriptions general and free of specific technologies. You will select the specific technologies for the design later in the concept design stage.

In the example on the next page, the implementations for the domestic Fortune 500 and medium/small business market segments proceed from the base platform through two extensions. The first phase of the design simplifies processes and provides unlimited access and help facilities, but does not support all ordering channels, nor does it support historical ordering data for all market segments. Subsequent phases of the design enhance the basic platform and increase the number of channels supported, as well as the amount of historical data stored in the system. The design is out-of-scope for the international customer segment because satisfying that segment would involve a new platform.

A Sample Multistage Plan

Design description / Market segment	Domestic Fortune 500	Domestic medium/small business	International customers
Phase 1 (4Q '00)	Streamlined process: Unlimited access and help facilities; Most channels supported; Limited history data	Streamlined process: Unlimited access and help facilities; Most channels supported; Limited history data	New platform TBD; Out of scope
Phase 2 (2Q '01)	Phase 1 platform with all requested channels supported	Phase 1 platform with all requested channels supported	New platform TBD; Out of scope
Phase 3 (4Q '01)	Phase 2 platform with all requested history data	Phase 2 platform with all requested history data	New platform TBD; Out of scope

2.5 Hold a Tollgate Review

Note: For general information on tollgate reviews, see section 1.5 in the Define step.

The tollgate review for the Measure step focuses on:

- The customer segmentation strategy.
- The top 10–15 customer needs.
- The top 8–10 CTQs and targets.
- Summarized benchmark information.
- The Multistage Plan.

This tollgate review can lead you to:

- Proceed to the Analyze step.
- Redo parts of the Measure step and hold another review.
- Stop the project.

How do I do it?

1. **Review the Tollgate Review Form used at the end of the Define step.**

2. **Revise and answer the specific questions that describe what was done in this step and what you will need to do in the Analyze step.**

   Tip Remember to update your Storyboard before proceeding to the Analyze step.

The Measure Tollgate Review Form

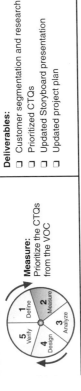

Measure:
Prioritize the CTQs
from the VOC

Deliverables:
- ☐ Customer segmentation and research
- ☐ Prioritized CTQs
- ☐ Updated Storyboard presentation
- ☐ Updated project plan

- Who are the customers of the process, product, or service? Of these, who are the most important customers?
- Do all customers have the same needs? If not, what are the different needs of the different segments?
- What data was collected and why? How did you collect the data?
- What are the prioritized CTQs? How did you determine this?
- What performance targets must the design meet to satisfy customers?
- How does your competition meet your customers' needs?
- What limitations or barriers have you encountered?
- Review your project plan: are you on track?
- What are your key learnings from the Measure step?
- What are your next steps?

Analyze
Concepts

Why do it?

To generate a range of concepts (i.e., ideas or solutions for the process, product, or service being designed), then evaluate and select the concept that best meets the CTQs within budget and resource constraints.

Tools used in this step:

- The QFD Matrix
- Creativity tools:
    - Brainstorming and Brainwriting
    - Analogies
    - Assumption Busting
    - The Morphological Box
- The Pugh Matrix
- Tollgate Review Forms

Outputs of this step:

- A selected concept (or concepts) for further analysis and design
- A tollgate review and updated Storyboard

Key questions answered in this step:

- What are the most important functions or processes that must be designed to meet the CTQs?

- What are the key inputs and outputs of each process?

- Which functions or processes require innovative new designs to maintain a competitive advantage?

- What are the possible design alternatives for each function or process?

- What criteria should we use to evaluate these design alternatives?

- How do we collect information on these criteria to help us effectively evaluate these designs?

- How does the selected concept affect the features included in the base design and platform extensions?

How do I do it?

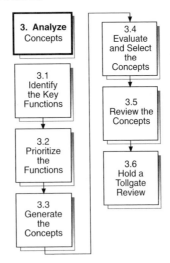

3. **Analyze** Concepts

3.1 Identify the Key Functions

3.2 Prioritize the Functions

3.3 Generate the Concepts

3.4 Evaluate and Select the Concepts

3.5 Review the Concepts

3.6 Hold a Tollgate Review

©2004 GOAL/QPC

3.1 Identify the Key Functions

1. **Express the process, product, or service to be designed as a "black box" with inputs and outputs.**

2. **Determine the functions or activities that have to be performed in the black box.**

   • The designed process, product, or service must perform certain activities (called functions) to provide value to the customer. As you design the process, product, or service, describe these functions in words that do not depend upon a specific technology, to prevent biasing your design toward that technology. For example, as you describe a process for cleaning clothes, describe the function as "remove dirt from clothes" rather than "wash clothes" because the term "wash" implies a specific technology. (The design must be able to perform the functions no matter what technology you use for the design.)

   • Express the functions in the most basic format, as a verb/noun pair.

   Caution: The wording of the functions is extremely important. Deciding too quickly on wording that implies specific technology and/or design decisions impedes the creative innovative process.

3. **Draw a block diagram showing the interactions between functions.**

   • Make sure that the outputs of the preceding functions lead into the inputs of the following functions and that no disconnected functions exist. Be aware that all functions may not be linearly connected.

4. **Draw a system boundary to define the limits for the process, product, or service to be designed.**

Tip For process or service design projects, the functions are identical to the process steps so the function diagram is simply a high-level process flowchart.

To identify the functions in an order placement process, for example, first express the process as a black box with inputs and outputs.

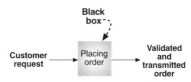

Next, use technology-independent words (such as "enter," "check," "confirm," and "transmit") to describe the functions or tasks to be performed in the black box. Express these functions as simply as possible. Show the interactions between the functions using arrows, and draw a dashed line to show the system boundary that defines the limits for the design.

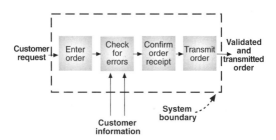

©2004 GOAL/QPC

3.2 Prioritize the Functions

1. **After identifying all of the key functions, identify those that are critical to the design to help you determine:**

   • Which functions need the most resources.

   • Which functions need innovative designs.

   • Which functions can use existing designs.

   • Which functions you can copy from competitors or industry standards.

2. **Prioritize the critical functions by mapping them to the CTQs using the QFD Matrix.**

   • Recall from the Measure step that the first QFD Matrix (QFD 1) uses the most important customer needs to prioritize the CTQs.

   A second QFD Matrix (QFD 2) will relate the CTQs prioritized in QFD 1 to the functions identified for the new design, to focus the design effort on the functions that will have the greatest impact. Also, with an understanding of the relationships between the CTQs and the functions, you can establish clear requirements for the critical functions to aid in developing more-detailed designs in the latter steps of the DMADV process.

   a) Place the CTQ measures from QFD 1 into Room 1 of QFD 2. Place the key functions you identified in substep 3.1 into Room 3 of QFD 2. Record the relationships between these functions and measures in the cells of Room 4 of QFD 2 by asking, "If we design this particular function correctly, what impact does it have on our ability to meet the CTQs?" Decide how strongly each function impacts each CTQ and use the 9, 3, 1 scale introduced in the Measure step to represent this relationship.

Caution: Be sure to ask the specific question, "If we design this particular function correctly, what impact does it have on our ability to meet the CTQs?" Reversing the question will skew the results.

b) Calculate the importance scores for each function by multiplying the importance ratings for the CTQs (from the "How important" row in QFD 1) by the 9, 3, 1 correlation rating you determined above for each cell, and then adding the cell scores in each column to calculate the importance score for each function. Record these scores in the "How important" row of Room 4 in QFD 2.

Tip Calculating the importance scores often results in large numbers that get even larger if you use these importance scores in further QFD Matrices. To reduce the size of these numbers, rescale the CTQ importance numbers by assigning a value of five to the most important CTQ and adjusting the other values accordingly.

Mapping the CTQs to the Functions of the Order Placement Process

QFD 2

CTQ measures	Order entry	Order processing	Order verification	Order transmittal	Importance of CTQs
Percentage of customer-desired technologies supported	9				68
Number of hours help facility is available	9				49
Number of process steps	9	9	9	9	57
Percentage of information about completed order status accessible by customer	9	9	9	9	50
Percentage of historical information not requiring reentry		9			57
Number of hours access is available	9				51
How important	2473	1476	963	963	

QFD 1

Customer needs	Percent of customer-desired technologies supported	Numbers of hours help facility is available	Number of process steps	Percent of information about complete and order status accessible by customer	Percent of historical information not requiring reentry	Number of hours access is available	How important
I need to place orders when I want						9	68
I need to place orders from any location	3						49
I need to be able to place orders using different technologies	9						57
I want an easily understandable process			3	3			50
I don't want to go through many steps			9	9			57
I want to know immediately if an order is confirmed				9			51
I need to be able to get help if I have questions	3	9		3		3	
How important	68	49	57	50	57	51	

The output of the QFD 2 Matrix is a prioritization of functions. This prioritization helps you identify the parts of the design that need to be innovative and the parts that can be supported by existing or "also-ran" technology. In our order placement process example, it is clear from the graphic above that order entry is the most important function and any process innovations should focus on this step of the order placement process.

> **Tip** Examine empty rows or columns in the QFD Matrix closely. A CTQ with no associated function (an empty row) may indicate that you did not identify all of the necessary functions. A function with no associated CTQ (an empty column) could be an example of a non-value-added function or a redundant function.

3. **After prioritizing the critical functions, review your Multistage Plan.**
   - Ask:
     - How many critical functions have been considered in the first phase of the design?
     - Are any critical functions not considered until later phases? What are the risk implications of this delay?
     - Have we left any functions out of the Multistage Plan? How should we include these functions?
     - Is it necessary to revise the Multistage Plan to adjust the platform descriptions for each phase?

3.3 Generate the Concepts

Concept generation involves creating as many alternative ideas or solutions for the process, product, or service as possible to meet customer requirements.

Tip Concept design is just one step toward building a process, product, or service. Proceeding step-by-step through the design process from concept to high-level to detailed design ensures that expensive, risky decisions are not made until you analyze the design in detail and there is a degree of confidence that the selected design will perform as required by the CTQs.

There are two approaches for generating concepts: *bottom up* and *top down*. The bottom-up approach generates concepts *function by function*. The top-down approach generates concepts *across* functions.

Tip The bottom-up approach works better for re-designing pieces of an existing process, product, or service, while the top-down approach is especially effective for new designs. However, many designs will incorporate some new design and some existing design together in a new process (i.e., an existing phone ordering process may need to utilize new technology, so part of the process will need a new design). If so, you may have to use a combination of approaches. For the part of the design that is a redesign, you can use a bottom-up approach. For the part of the design that is new, you should work top down. Ultimately, you will have to combine these two approaches as you complete your work.

When generating concepts using either a bottom-up or top-down approach, make sure that you include all of the following applicable elements in the concept description:

- Product features
- Information systems
- Human systems
- All key processes

- Materials
- Equipment
- Facilities

Tip Do not worry too much about using the exact categories listed above. Use this list only as a guide to ensure that you have not missed anything in the process of generating concepts.

To generate concepts in a *bottom-up approach*:

1. Determine whether you need to create a new design for each function or whether an existing design is adequate.

2. For each function that needs a new design, generate as many verbal descriptions or drawings of alternate solutions as possible.

3. Eliminate or combine impractical alternatives for each function until no more than 3–5 viable options for each function remain.

   - Note that these alternatives are not concepts; concepts involve combining the alternatives across functions.

4. Assemble concepts by determining which alternatives will combine well with alternatives of other functions, and then linking compatible alternatives together to create concepts or design solutions.

5. Select 3–5 concepts for further analysis.

   Note: The most common tool to generate concepts in a bottom-up approach is the Morphological Box, which is explained in greater detail later in this chapter.

A bottom-up approach (using a Morphological Box) for our order placement process will generate alternatives for each key function identified in the black box from substep 3.1, as shown on the next page.

©2004 GOAL/QPC

A Bottom-Up Concept Generation Example

Function	Alternative 1	Alternative 2
Enter order	Over the telephone using an Interactive Voice Response (IVR) system	Over the internet using a secure browser ★
Check for errors	Manual check using a live agent	System check for completed fields ★
Confirm order receipt	Follow-up telephone call	Email ★
Transmit order	Order carried to delivery department by agent	Order information accessed over intranet ★

—⊙— Concept 1   —★— Concept 2

You could conceivably assemble sixteen different concepts $(2 \times 2 \times 2 \times 2 = 16)$ by combining these alternatives. After developing the sixteen concepts, you would then select 3–5 concepts for further study. The concepts you select must be feasible and, based on informed judgment, deemed worthy of further study.

To generate concepts in a *top-down approach*:

1. **Develop concept ideas at a systems level (across all functions) to show how you could satisfy customer needs.**

   • Envision an entire system that will satisfy the requirements of your customers.

2. **Write verbal descriptions of these concepts or draw the concepts as pictures.**

3. **Map the verbal descriptions or drawings to the necessary functions.**

4. **Ensure you have not missed any critical functions.**

5. **Mark the functions that need a new design.**

A top-down approach for our order placement process could generate the following three concept examples:

Top-Down Concept Generation Examples

Concept 1: **Automated telephone ordering**

Customers can call the order processing center twenty-four hours a day and can place their order without human intervention. Confirmation is immediately available upon completion of the ordering steps. Customers can obtain verbal information about any ordering questions by pushing the appropriate telephone buttons. Customers can also fax or mail in their orders to the order processing center, but confirmation is not immediately available. Customers seeking confirmation for such orders or information about previous orders can call the twenty-four-hour order processing center. All questions are addressed by this single center. Orders are stored in a database accessible by the order management department.

Concept 2: **Internet ordering with videoconferencing support**

Customers have a virtual account that they can access over the internet. The virtual account provides information about current and past orders and also provides access to questions about ordering. For additional questions, videoconferencing with a live agent is available at an additional charge; for customers who do not have videoconferencing capabilities, regular telephone communication is available and the customer's screen is visible to the agent. Customers can call, fax, or mail non-internet orders to an order processing center twenty-four hours a day. Confirmation is available immediately on orders called in, but not on orders written or faxed. Orders are stored in an intranet database accessible by the order management department.

Concept 3: **Point-of-sale connection to an order manager**

An order manager is linked to the customer's point-of-sale system and an order is automatically placed based on store stock levels. Confirmation of orders is provided automatically to customers when the order is placed. Overrides of automatic orders or questions about previous orders are called into the order processing center. Fax and written orders are not supported.

Both the top-down and bottom-up approach require some creative thinking in the actual generation of concepts. Begin with benchmarking techniques that study designs in competing and noncompeting businesses and then use creative idea-generation techniques that focus on analogies, connections, extrapolations, and creative visualization, to develop new ideas.

The skills you will need to creatively generate ideas include domain relevant skills (knowledge of the facts, technical skills, and motor skills), creativity relevant skills (experience with creativity tools and a disciplined work style), and task motivation. Typically, the creativity relevant skills provide an extra "push" to a person or team possessing domain relevant skills. Creativity alone cannot substitute for a lack of subject matter knowledge or motivation.

> **Note:** In the Measure step, you may have benchmarked for measures and technical comparisons. In the Analyze step, you will benchmark to understand *how* world-class organizations provide products or services. The best practices of other organizations provide ideas for concepts at this stage of design.

There are several kinds of creativity tools, including:

- Association Methods: Tools such as Brainstorming and Brainwriting that build upon what you already know.

- Creative Confrontation Methods: Tools such as Analogies that challenge what you think you know.

- Assumption Busting Methods: Tools that challenge the assumptions or perspectives you currently have.

- Analytic Systematic Methods: Tools such as the Morphological Box that provide systematic guidance in constructing innovative concepts.

Note: For more information on creativity tools, see *Product Design: Fundamentals and Methods* by N.J.M. Roozenburg , J. Eekels, and N.F.M. Roozenburg, Wiley, 1996, and *The Creativity Tools Memory Jogger*™ by Michael Brassard and Diane Ritter, GOAL/QPC, 1999.

What is it?

Brainstorming allows team members to build on each other's creativity while staying focused on their joint mission. It encourages open thinking when a team is stuck in "the same old way of thinking," gets all team members involved, and prevents a few people from dominating the whole group.

There are two major methods for brainstorming: *Structured Brainstorming* in which each team member gives an idea in turn, and *Unstructured Brainstorming* in which team members give ideas as they come to mind.

Why use it?

To allow a team to creatively and efficiently generate a high volume of ideas on any topic by creating a process that is free of criticism and judgment

How do I do it?

1. **Agree on a central Brainstorming question and write it down for everyone to see.**

   • Be sure that everyone understands the question, issue, or problem. Check this understanding by asking one or two members to paraphrase it before recording it on a flipchart or board.

2. Have each team member, in turn, give an idea.

- Allow a team member to pass at any time. (While the rotation process encourages full participation, it may also heighten anxiety for inexperienced or shy team members.)

Tip The Unstructured Brainstorming process is the same as the Structured method except that everyone gives ideas at any time, rather than in turns. There is no need to "pass" because ideas are not solicited in turn.

Caution: Do not allow criticism of any idea. Criticism impedes the creative process and may prevent team members from sharing their ideas.

3. As you generate ideas, write each one in large, visible letters on a flipchart or other writing surface.

- Make sure you record every idea in the exact words of the speaker; don't interpret his or her meaning. To ensure that you have captured the speaker's exact meaning, ask the speaker if the idea has been worded accurately.

4. Continue to generate ideas until each person passes (or discussion stops, if you are using the Unstructured method), indicating that the ideas have been exhausted.

- Keep the process moving and relatively short; 5–20-minute sessions work well, depending on how complex the topic is.

Note: Brainstorming to generate concepts may require more than twenty minutes and/or more than one Brainstorming session.

5. **Review the written list of ideas for clarity and discard any duplicates.**

   • Discard an idea only if it is truly a duplicate. It is often important to preserve subtle differences that are revealed in slightly different wordings.

   Tip For effective brainstorming:

   • Allow individuals to complete their thoughts.

   • Build on existing ideas.

   • Be brief when stating an idea.

   • Organize, categorize, and evaluate only after the session.

   • Strive for quantity.

   • Don't criticize ideas or make judgments as ideas are being offered.

   • Don't dominate the session.

An alternative way to stimulate creative team thinking is through Brainwriting. There are two approaches to Brainwriting: the 6-3-5 Method and the Brainwriting Pool.

In the 6-3-5 Method, six participants each write three ideas on a separate form. The participants pass the forms among themselves five times, adding new ideas to the forms.

In the Brainwriting Pool, 5–8 participants each jot ideas on a sheet of paper in silence. Participants who have run out of ideas place their sheets in the middle of the table, pick up another member's sheet, and add ideas to it. After 20–30 minutes, the ideas are collected and evaluated.

What is it?

An analogy uses a random word, object, or situation to make unusual connections to a problem or design challenge. It provides a virtually unlimited supply of inspiration for breakthrough thinking, enables team members to create a new focus point for their thinking, and re-energizes a Brainstorming process that has reached a lull.

Why use it?

To stimulate fresh perspectives and new solutions by using random words, pictures, or situations that are unrelated to the original problem.

How do I do it?

1. **Start with a familiar situation and make it strange by deliberately altering or undermining it in some way.**

   • Alter it by using analogies such as:

   - A personal analogy (i.e., put yourself in the problem).

   - A direct analogy (i.e., seek an comparable problem from another discipline).

   - A symbolic analogy (i.e., explain the problem using symbols or metaphors).

   - An ideal analogy (i.e., imagine an ideal situation).

2. **Adjust these analogies to fit the original problem.**

   • Apply the thinking associated with the analogy to the original problem to stimulate new ways to solve the problem.

Assumption Busting

What is it?

Assumption Busting challenges the conventional assumptions about a problem or issue.

Why use it?

To escape the self-imposed constraints that traditional assumptions often create

How do I do it?

1. State the problem or design challenge.

2. Write down as many existing assumptions about the problem or design challenge as you can think of.

3. Challenge the assumption by:

   a) **Reversing the assumption.** For example, if you currently assume that all transactions require approval from a department head, assume that such approval will no longer be required.

   b) **Modifying the assumption to make it better or easier to deal with**. Change a name, time frame, or location. For example, assume that supervisors, rather than department heads, need to approve transactions.

   c) **Varying your perspective**. Try viewing the assumptions from the perspective of another person, work group, or organization and describe the problem from their perspective. Write down new ideas that emerge from looking at things this way.

What is it?

A Morphological Box helps identify all of the parts of the problem that you must address to create a successful solution. It displays options for solving each essential part of the problem, and helps you evaluate several solutions at one time.

Why use it?

To provide a more systematic means of generating solutions

How do I do it?

1. **Assemble a knowledgeable team.**

   • Unlike some of the other creativity tools, the Morphological Box requires experts in the content area being discussed. These experts can join the team as needed or become permanent members.

2. **Define the parameters necessary for any solution to the problem.**

   • A parameter is a characteristic that a solution must possess for it to be effective. A good parameter must:

     – Be independent from the other parameters.

     – Describe a complete solution when combined with the other parameters.

     – Be valid for all potential solutions.

     – Represent an essential characteristic of an effective solution.

Tip While there is no absolute rule for the number of parameters you can use, you should work from a list of six parameters or fewer when starting out. If you have difficulty identifying the parameters, create an Affinity Diagram for the design challenge and use the headers developed in the Affinity Diagram as the parameters.

3. **Place the selected parameters in the left-hand column of a matrix. Label the successive columns of the matrix as "Alternative 1," "Alternative 2," and so on.**

    Tip You will have a good list of parameters when you can "add" all of the parameters together to get a complete solution.

4. **Generate options (alternatives) for each parameter.**

    • Brainstorm a minimum of two options for each parameter.

    Caution: More options are not always better. Generate options that draw on both your current knowledge and your imagination.

5. **Build alternative solutions by linking different options.**

    • Within each parameter (row), select at least one option. You can make this selection randomly (to maximize creative combinations) or systematically (to intentionally focus on specific combinations).

    Note: Generally, only one option is selected within a parameter. Select more than one option only when it will lead to more-interesting combinations. Don't choose more options simply to avoid making a choice.

- Clearly mark the selected option(s) within the first parameter and draw a line to the selected option(s) in the next parameter. Continue to repeat this process until you connect all selected options by a line.

- Develop alternative combinations of options by repeating the marking and connecting process. Distinguish between the combinations of options by using differently marked points (e.g., boxes, triangles, circles) and connecting lines (e.g., solid, dotted, dashed). Be creative but also be clear.

6. **Analyze the alternative solutions and select the best one(s).**

Methods to evaluate and analyze the combinations include:

- Intuitive: Selecting those combinations of options that "feel" the most promising or interesting. (This works best with six parameters or fewer.)

- Optimization: Selecting the "best" option within each parameter and then combining these options to produce the one "best" combination across all parameters. Understand that the resulting combination may not actually work and may require substituting some options with the next best option to create a viable solution.

- Sequential: Considering the two, three, or four most important parameters and their options, then selecting options for each of the remaining parameters that look like the best combination with the options chosen for the most important parameters.

Tip Even a modest-sized Morphological Box can generate a large number of different combinations. (To determine the number of possible combinations, multiply the number of options in the first parameter by the number of options in the second parameter, by the number in the third parameter, and so on, to the last parameter.) Clearly, the sheer number of possible combinations that a Morphological Box can create demonstrates a need to narrow down the number of combinations for evaluation.

A Sample Morphological Box

Parameters	Alternative 1	Alternative 2	Alternative 3	Alternative 4
Voice of the Customer	Interviews	Question-naires	Joint QFD project	Historical data
Selecting the priority/ focus	Spread 100 points	Analytical Hierarchy Process	Customer voting	Weighting principles
Concept generation	7 Creativity Tools	TRIZ/ Patent search	Research	Competitor analysis
Concept selection	Boss decides	Pugh's new concept selection	Dart board	Criteria
Taking cost out	Dropping features	Value engineering/ trimming	Activity-based costing	Customer input
Improving reliability	Forced failure (TRIZ)	Fault Tree Analysis	Failure Mode & Effects Analysis	Robust Design (Taguchi)

—○— Concept 1   —★— Concept 2

3.4 Evaluate and Select the Concepts

In the previous substep, you generated a number of solutions or concepts for your design. Now you must evaluate these options and select one or two concepts for further development.

One way to consolidate the ideas you generated is through controlled convergence. Controlled convergence is a process that successively generates and reduces concepts until a satisfactory concept is reached. Each round of the controlled convergence process reduces the number of remaining concepts until only one or two remain.

Controlled Convergence

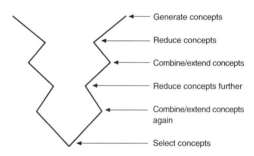

Tip As you proceed through controlled convergence, do not generate completely new concepts to add to the existing set. Instead, combine and extend what you have already created to produce a smaller set of superior concepts.

You can also use a Pugh Matrix to help you evaluate and select design concepts.

What is it?

The Pugh Matrix helps select the best design concept(s) from among alternatives.

Why use it?

To produce more-innovative and robust designs by comparing design concepts and integrating the best features from various concepts into "super concepts"

How do I do it?

1. Determine a baseline for the project.

- For redesign projects, use the current process, product, or service as the baseline. For new designs, select the "middle of the road" (i.e., neither too manual nor requiring extremely advanced technology) as a baseline.

2. Place the concepts as the headers in the columns of a matrix and list the evaluation criteria in the matrix rows.

- Use customer CTQs from the QFD Matrix as your evaluation criteria and add other business criteria such as cost, ease of implementation, and technological feasibility.

3. Compare each concept to the baseline on each criterion.

- If the concept is better than the baseline on the criterion, assign a "+"; if it is worse, assign a "-"; if it is the same, assign an "S."

---

4. Count the number of positives, negatives, and "sames" for each concept and record them in the matrix.

5. Calculate the weighted sums for the positives by adding together the importance ratings for each criterion assigned a "+". Calculate the weighted sums of the negatives by adding together the importance ratings for each criterion assigned a "-". Record these sums in the matrix.

   • Use the importance ratings for the CTQs from the QFD 1 Matrix. If necessary, rescale these importance ratings for convenience.

6. Compare the total weighted score (the weighted sum of the positives minus the weighted sum of the negatives) for each column to help you select the best concepts.

   Tip Use the concept generation process and the Pugh Matrix in repeated rounds to help develop "super concepts." To develop these super concepts, after the first round of ranking, create new concepts by:

   • Synthesizing the best features of the different alternatives into new concepts.

   • Enhancing the strongest concepts by adding features from the unselected concepts to address weak areas.

   Follow this second round of concept generation with another round of ranking using the Pugh Matrix. Repeat this concept generation/concept selection process until you have one or two new super concepts that emerge during this process.

A Sample Pugh Matrix

CTQs from QFD 1	Baseline (Current process)	Telephone ordering	Internet ordering	Point-of-sale connection	Importance rating
Percentage of customer-desired technologies supported	S	S	S	-	68
Number of hours help facility is available	S	S	S	S	49
Number of process steps	S	S	S	+	57
Percentage of information directly accessible by customer	S	S	+	-	50
Percentage of historical information not requiring reentry	S	S	+	+	57
Number of hours access is available	S	S	S	S	51
Sum of positives	0	0	2	2	
Sum of negatives	0	0	0	2	
Sum of sames	6	6	4	2	
Weighted sum of positives	0	0	107	114	
Weighted sum of negatives	0	0	0	118	
Total weighted score	0	0	107	-4	

Concept Selection Legend: Better = +   Same = S   Worse = -

©2004 GOAL/QPC

3.5 Review the Concepts

A design review objectively evaluates the quality of a design at various stages of the design process. It provides an opportunity for voices external to the design team (including those of the customers) to provide feedback on the design as you develop the process, product, or service.

A well-conducted design review ensures that the design will satisfy customers and the design process will function effectively to produce a high-quality process, product, or service.

Design reviews are quality control tools applied to the design process. They ensure the effectiveness of the design (i.e., the features provided by the design will meet customers' aesthetic and performance needs) and the efficiency of the design process (i.e., the teams responsible for the various elements of the design are working in a coordinated fashion that minimizes rework and duplicated efforts).

> *Tip* Design reviews are different from tollgate reviews. Design reviews focus on obtaining input on the design from outside of the design team at several key stages during the design process. Tollgate reviews focus on the design methodology and overall project issues and risks at the end of each step in the design process and whenever significant project problems or risks are identified.

When conducting a design review, remember to:

- Ensure that the design review gets both internal and external input.

- Focus on identifying and resolving problems during the reviews, and use the feedback you receive to make changes immediately to the design.

Tip Projects may have different places in the design process where a design review is needed. Organize a design review whenever external feedback appears appropriate or when there are co-ordination issues. Conduct multiple design reviews at any stage necessary to ensure the quality of the process, product, or service. It is especially important to conduct:

- A concept review after identifying one or two key concepts and determining their feasibility.

- A high-level design review after designing and testing a selected concept to some level of detail but before beginning the detailed design.

- A pre-pilot design review after completing the detailed design, but before the process, product, or service is ready to be piloted.

A concept review obtains feedback from customers and other interested parties (other organizational entities, suppliers, etc.) about the concepts that were selected. The feedback obtained during the concept review is a critical check on the design team's thinking. It can provide insights that lead to modifications of the selected concept(s) early in the design process when changes are easier to make and risks and costs can be minimized.

How do I do it?

1. **Determine the evaluation criteria and targets.**

- Develop evaluation criteria for the concepts from the CTQs and any other constraints identified in the Pugh Matrix. Consider:

  - Completeness (i.e., which functions are included in the concept and which are excluded?).

  - Performance (i.e., how does the concept perform against the most important CTQs?).

- Operating details (i.e., how will the customers/ organization/suppliers interact with the product or service described in the concept?).

- Aesthetics (i.e., how does the process, product, or service look and feel? How does the operating environment look and feel? How comfortable and safe do customers feel when using the process, product, or service?).

- Cost (i.e., what is the approximate cost of delivering the process, product, or service?).

Tip Develop very specific criteria. The more specific the criteria, the more precise the feedback can be.

2. **Select the participants for the design review.**

• Be sure to select a small number of participants whose feedback is critical and who will provide honest and constructive feedback. Focus on participants who will help identify all of the factors that may affect the success of the design in the market. Include:

- Key customers (about 10–15 customers).

- Technology innovators: Those whose views may represent future trends in the industry.

- High-volume users: Those who are likely to purchase a large amount of the product or service if the design meets their needs.

- Pilot partners: Those who may be willing to try out the process, product, or service during the pilot.

- Early adopters.

- The general public.

- Key suppliers (2–3 suppliers).

- Key stakeholders and senior leadership.

Tip Not all customer groups may be relevant for all projects. Also, because the number of customers is small, be sure to carefully distinguish individual viewpoints from general themes. Different customer groups may have different preferred concepts; you may need to balance different viewpoints and preferences.

3. **Develop design review checklists and evaluation sheets.**

   • Proper documentation is critical for both describing the design and collecting feedback. Be sure to include the following types of documents in your concept review:

     - A review agenda and format that details how you will conduct the review and describes the important steps that you must cover

     - A concept depiction that may include descriptions on paper, drawings, photographs, prototypes, models, blueprints, data, calculations, and anything else that will help explain the concept to the participants

     - A data collection checklist that lists the data that you need to collect for all of the key aspects of the design and consists of sampling schemes, formats, surveys, questionnaires, guides, and other documents that support data collection

     - An improvement checklist that lists the findings in order of priority, lists the actions that you need to take to make corrections where needed, identifies the owners for these actions, and sets up times by which these actions need to be completed

4. **Collect and analyze the data.**

   • Because there are only a small number of participants in a design review, be sure to collect data from multiple sources to provide a broad range of data and depth to the feedback, including:

- Verbal descriptions of the participants' impression of the concepts.

- Videotapes of participants interacting with the product or service.

- A ranking or rating by the participants of the attributes of each concept.

- A ranking of overall concepts.

• Several types of data analysis may be appropriate depending on the type of data you collected. You can conduct analysis of both qualitative responses to questionnaires/interviews and quantitative data from surveys. (In practice, most data analysis is qualitative.) Typical types of analyses include:

- An in-depth video analysis to identify common difficulties that customers face in using the process, product, or service.

- Qualitative data analysis of verbal data to identify common themes about customer likes and dislikes.

- Statistical analysis (if possible) to quantify priorities and preferences.

5. **Identify and document actions based on data analysis.**

• Answer the following questions, based on the results of the data analysis:

- Is there a clearly preferred concept?

- If not, are there particular preferred attributes belonging to different concepts that we can combine to create a single preferred concept?

- If there is a preferred concept, do we need additional analyses to resolve concerns and issues?

- Who is responsible for the resolution of key items and when?

- Is there a need for another concept review?

6. **Debrief the concept review session for future learnings.**

   • Note what worked and what didn't work in the design review session to improve future sessions.

   Caution: Of all of the design reviews, participants in concept reviews tend to be the most critical because much of the design is still in the idea stage. Do not get discouraged or annoyed with the criticism or ignore the feedback from a concept review. Ignoring feedback is the most common cause of a failed review session. Other causes of failed sessions include:

   • Poor or inadequate preparation.

   • Poor or inadequate documentation.

   • Discouraging open and frank communication.

   • Selecting only "friendly" participants.

   • Not having the right design team members.

   If, unfortunately, you experience a failed session, the debriefing will be a critical component for moving forward. After the debriefing, you may find that you need to adjust the concept(s) and perform an additional concept review before continuing the DMADV process.

3.6 Hold a Tollgate Review

Note: For general information on tollgate reviews, see section 1.5 in the Define step.

Before moving from the Analyze step on to high-level design, be sure to hold a tollgate review.

The tollgate review for the Analyze step focuses on:

- A list of key functions.
- A list of top concepts.
- The Pugh Matrix.
- The concept review outputs.
- A risk analysis update.

This tollgate review can lead you to:

- Proceed to the Design step.
- Redo your work on concepts, the concept review, and the tollgate review.
- Stop the project.

How do I do it?

1. **Update the Storyboard.**

2. **Present a progress report at the tollgate meeting using the Tollgate Review Form.**
   - Review and revise the Tollgate Review Form used at the end of the Measure step.

3. **Discuss the progress report and any issues that arise. Ask and answer questions about data and logic.**

4. **Identify the strengths and weaknesses of the project so far.**
   - Identify the strengths and weaknesses in using the DMADV methodology.

5. **Decide on the next steps for the project.**

6. **Identify the strengths and weaknesses of the concept review.**

The Analyze Tollgate Review Form

Deliverables:

- ☐ List of key functions
- ☐ List of top concepts
- ☐ Selected concept
- ☐ Updated risk plan
- ☐ Updated Storyboard presentation
- ☐ Updated project plan

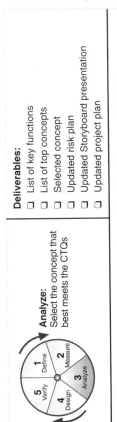

Analyze:
Select the concept that best meets the CTQs

- What are the most important functions that must be designed to meet the CTQs?
- Which parts of the process, product, or service require innovative new designs to maintain a competitive advantage?
- What are the top concepts developed (for each function)?
- What criteria did you use to evaluate and select the best concept?
- What are the risks associated with each concept?
- Does the project charter require any revisions?
- What limitations or barriers have you encountered?
- Review your project plan; are you on track?
- What are your key learnings from the Analyze step?
- What are your next steps?

©2004 GOAL/QPC

Why do it?

To develop high-level and detailed designs, test the design components, and prepare for the pilot and full-scale deployment.

Tools used in this step:

- The QFD Matrix
- Simulation
- Prototyping
- The Design Scorecard
- Failure Mode and Effects Analysis (FMEA)/Error Mode and Effects Analysis (EMEA)
- Planning tools
- The Process Management Chart
- Tollgate Review Forms

Note: Additional resources for these tools can be found in the Appendix.

Outputs of this step:

- A tested and approved high-level design
- A tested and approved detailed design
- A detailed, updated risk assessment

- A plan for conducting the pilot
- Completed design reviews and approvals
- A tollgate review and updated Storyboard

Key questions answered in this step:
- What are the key design elements that the final design must include?
- How do we prioritize these design elements?
- How can we distribute the design work among sub-teams?
- How do we ensure that these sub-teams communicate effectively with each other during the design process?
- At what point will we "freeze" the design?
- How do we test the design to ensure that it will work before implementation?
- How do we identify weak points in the design that may be susceptible to failure?
- How do we plan the pilot to ensure that it is realistic and produces meaningful results?

How do I do it?

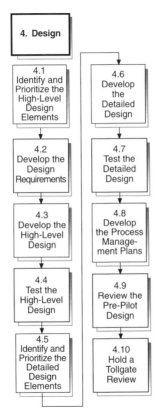

The Design step encompasses both *high-level design* and *detailed design*. This two-phased high-level/detailed design approach allows you to:

- Make decisions about the major design *components* and how they fit together before expending effort and money on detailed decisions, resulting in a more-stable and robust design.

- Evaluate the *performance and feasibility* of the high-level design before spending more resources on the detailed design (to make the design process more cost-effective and efficient).

- Better understand the *risks* associated with the design.

    Tip The overall approach to developing both high-level and detailed design is the same; only the level of specificity differs. The high-level design includes enough detail to allow you to evaluate the design's performance and feasibility. (You may need to test several high-level design alternatives before selecting a suitable design.) The detailed design further develops the selected high-level design to enable you to test and implement the design.

    This process is truly repetitive in nature; after selecting a high-level design, you repeat the design steps until you reach a level of detail sufficient to pilot a solution.

The challenge of the design process is to make choices that simultaneously balance the benefit, cost, and risk elements and that are compatible with previous strategic decisions.

©2004 GOAL/QPC

4.1 Identify and Prioritize the High-Level Design Elements

How do I do it?

1. **Identify the high-level design elements.**

   The design elements are the basic descriptions of the components needed to make the process, product, or service work. They answer "what is needed."

   It may help to think of and describe the design elements in categories. Common categories to consider include:

   • Product/service elements.
   • Process elements.
   • Information systems elements.
   • Human systems elements.
   • Equipment.
   • Materials/supplies.
   • Facilities.

   Tip You may not need to include all of the elements listed above in your design; use this list of elements simply to ensure that your design is complete and includes everything you need to be successful.

   Using the list of design elements to ensure completeness in the design will also remind you to integrate the design of products with related processes, in a process called *product and process planning*. In addition to meeting customer requirements, the product must interface well with relevant processes such as manufacturing, packaging, distribution, and technical support, and it must fit well with suppliers' processes.

Designing the products and processes together allows:

- Process capabilities to be addressed or taken into account by the overall design.

- Inspection, wait, transport, and rework steps to be minimized by the design.

- Data collection for ongoing monitoring to be designed into the process.

To identify all of the necessary process elements for the design, follow the product or service as it would actually flow through the organization. Once you have mapped the path through the organization, identify value-added and non-value-added areas in the process to show where you will need to redesign current processes, and analyze gaps in the design to identify where you will need to create interfaces with existing processes.

> **Tip** When redesigning a process, product, or service, you may be able to reuse some parts of an existing design; in such cases, you may only need to design the new elements and interfaces. Even with new designs, you may be able to use "off-the-shelf" or existing designs for the least important elements; you may need to create innovative or breakthrough designs only for the most important elements.

The design elements for our multichannel order placement process could include:

- The order processing equipment.
- The order process itself.
- Order processing agents.
- An order processing facility.

©2004 GOAL/QPC

Design Elements for the
Order Placement Process

Element category	Element description
Product	• Order entry form
Process	• Order placement process
Information systems	• Interactive Voice Response (IVR) scripts • Order processing system/database
Human systems	• Order processing agents
Equipment	• Fax • Phone network • IVR hardware
Materials/supplies	• A list of materials and supplies
Facilities	• Order processing center

2. **Prioritize the design elements to determine which are the most important ones to focus on.**

   • Use a QFD Matrix (QFD 3) to help you focus on the design elements that will have the greatest impact. (The most important design elements will impact the most important functions, and understanding the relationship between CTQs, functions, and design elements will help establish clear requirements for the critical design elements.)

   - Create the QFD 3 Matrix with the functions in the rows and the design elements in the columns. (When designing products, you may need a separate QFD Matrix for each design element category.) For each element/function relationship, ask, "To what extent does this element impact the design's ability to perform this function?" Use the 9, 3, 1 scale you used previously to record the strength of the relationship and use matrix multiplication to help summarize your answers.

Tip In product applications, the objective of the linked QFD Matrices is to formally deploy requirements (quantitative specifications) from the CTQs to the functions to the design elements. For service or process applications, the QFD Matrices follow a more informal approach to primarily help you to determine where to focus your design efforts. Service and process applications will often use a total of only two or three QFD Matrices to establish the CTQ linkage down to the functional level. Manufacturing and engineering design applications may require more QFD Matrices to establish the CTQ linkages from the high-level customer needs to the component level of the design.

QFD 3 Matrix
for the Order Placement Process

Functions \ High-Level Design Elements	Order entry form	Order placement process	Business rules applications	Order processing agents	Order processing system/database	Order processing center	Multichannel switch	Application servers	Importance of functions
Enter order	9	9	9	3	9		9	9	4.2
Check for errors	3	9		9		1			2.5
Confirm order receipt		9	9	9			3	9	1.6
Transmit order		9			9	1	9		1.6
How important	45	89	52	50	52	10	57	52	

This example matrix shows that the order placement process itself is the most important high-level design element (which is typical for service applications because the process drives the design). Because this is an application involving the internet, the switch and the internet application hardware and software are also important, followed by the order processing agents (who are primarily available for backup support), the supplies, and, lastly, the facilities.

The information in this matrix is particularly valuable. Typically, teams place a lot of emphasis on the technology in the design and do not spend much time designing the process itself. But without a good process, the technology cannot function adequately. By using a QFD Matrix such as the one on the previous page, the importance of the "work" process (the order placement process) becomes evident and the need to focus on it, as well as the technology, is clear.

4.2 Develop the Design Requirements

The design requirements are the quantitative performance specifications for each element of the design. They describe how the design elements must perform to allow the designed process, product, or service to meet the CTQs. They answer "how much of each element is needed" and "how each design element should perform," to help you select the most appropriate design alternatives for implementation.

Note: The performance requirements for functions and elements resemble CTQs in that there is a measure with a target and specifications for the measure, but these requirements are more specific than the CTQs.

How do I do it?

1. Develop the design requirements by quantitatively modeling the relationship between the output performance requirements of the design (the CTQs that the design team developed in the Measure step) and the process or input variables that impact the output performance.

    Tip When designing a new product, include de-

©2004 GOAL/QPC

signs-for-manufacturability, designs-for-reliability, designs-for-maintainability, and designs-for-life-cycle cost. These will add requirements that flow through the entire design process and should be considered when developing design requirements.

- Use the $y = f(x)$ formula to describe the relationships between the CTQs and the process variables that impact the CTQs.

The $y = f(x)$ formula states that an output (y) is a function (f) of the variables (x) that directly affect the output. Here, the output performance requirements of the design (the CTQs) constitute the y and the design element requirements that impact the CTQs comprise the x. The $y = f(x)$ formula is a simple way to illustrate the causal relationship between the CTQs and the design elements, and to show which variables or inputs you will need to control to ensure that the design will meet the performance requirements.

Tip The output performance (y) can be a function of many variables (x_1, x_2, x_3, etc.) that will impact performance.

$$y = f(x_1, x_2, x_3, \ldots x_n)$$

- There are three levels of $y = f(x)$ relationships:
  - The strategic level (i.e., how the performance of each major service attribute [x] affects the performance of the business [y])
  - The service level (i.e., how the performance of each process [x] affects the performance of the service attribute [y])
  - The process level (i.e., how the performance of the process steps/functions [x] affects the performance of each process [y])

Note that the measures and requirements at different levels are linked. The y's of the lower levels become the x's of each successively higher level as you proceed from the process level to the strategic level.

Order Placement Process Example

Level	$y = f(x)$ relationship
Strategic level	Market share = f (satisfaction with order processing, satisfaction with service delivery, satisfaction with customer service, satisfaction with billing)
Service level	Satisfaction with order processing = f (percentage of customer technologies supported, number of process steps, percentage of historical information not requiring reentry)
Process level	Percentage of historical information not requiring reentry = f (percentage of database capacity used for historical information)

The example shows that, at the strategic level, market share is influenced by customers' satisfaction with various aspects of the service. Satisfaction with each aspect of the service (the service level) depends upon the performance of each aspect relative to key CTQs (e.g., the satisfaction with order processing depends on the performance of the order processing process relative to the CTQs identified by the design team in the Measure step). Finally, the performance of each process (the process level) depends upon the design elements that make up the process and the performance specifications of the design elements.

©2004 GOAL/QPC

Tip For high-level and detailed design, *focus on the process level relationships* (because they deal with design elements and performance specifications). Develop these process level relationships using:

- Business knowledge.
- Benchmarks and analogies.
- Trials and prototypes.
- Experiments.
- Simulations.
- Data analysis.

- Use $y = f(x)$ relationships to develop the design requirements for all of the important design elements identified in the QFD 3 Matrix. The design requirements could specify a particular design alternative, a performance requirement for the element, or the number of units of a particular element needed for the design.

Tip There is no magic to developing the $y = f(x)$ relationships. To develop these relationships, you simply need data on the input variables and the output.

When redesigning a process, product, or service, you can develop design requirements using data from existing processes. However, with new designs, input and output data is often not easily available, so you must use a combination of methods to compile this data. Business knowledge, coupled with benchmarks from comparable processes, can serve as initial guides for defining these relationships. If you require more-precise definitions (such as in high-risk designs), you may need to collect data using demonstrations, testing, or limited trials to estimate these design requirements. Simulations (explained in greater detail later in this chapter) can also help in identifying $y = f(x)$ relationships in situations where precise data does not exist.

When developing $y = f(x)$ relationships:

- Select only key CTQs.

- Select only unusual/complex relationships to model.

- Simplify the $y = f(x)$ relationships to include only the most important input factors.

- Use benchmarks, analogies, and existing data where possible.

A Graphical Representation of a
$y = f(x)$ Relationship with Diminishing Returns

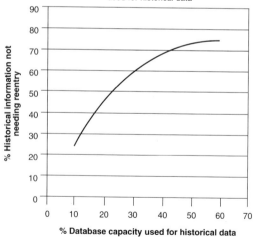

CTQ = Percentage of historical data not needing reentry

Design requirement = Percentage of database capacity used for historical data

In this example, the capacity of the database needed to store historical information (the design requirement, x) increases nonlinearly with the amount of data not needing reentry (the CTQ, y), possibly because the complexity of the historical data increases after a few basic pieces of historical information have been stored. Recall from the work in the Measure step (summarized in the QFD 1 Matrix) that the target for the percentage of historical information not requiring reentry is 90%; clearly this present database is incapable of meeting this requirement. A larger database or one with a different storage algorithm must be found.

> **Tip** In some cases, it may help to develop an intermediate level of requirements (between the concept level requirements and the design element requirements) before you determine the requirements for the high-level design, especially if the relationships are complex or if only some of the elements are being designed. This "design decomposition" is also useful if different teams are responsible for different aspects of the design. (This approach is more common for the design of products and is less critical for the design of services or processes.)

> **Caution:** Developing the performance requirements for elements is often difficult and time-consuming. Enlist the help of experts knowledgeable about the process, product, or service, and experts in statistics, if necessary.

> **Tip** You can also use Design of Experiments (DOE) to explore the relationships between multiple process variables and the output performance requirements. DOE is a systematic method to aggressively learn about a process, product, or service by manipulating multiple settings in the design. DOE can help you:
>
> • Identify the factors that affect the performance measures.
>
> • Test cause-and-effect theories.

- Understand the relationships among design factors.
- Optimize process, product, and service designs.
- Design robust processes, products, and services.
- Improve your ability to manufacture the design.
- Improve the reliability of the design.

Note: An in-depth explanation of DOE is beyond the scope of this book. For more information, consult *The Six Sigma Memory Jogger™ II* or *The Black Belt Memory Jogger™*.

Design Element Performance Requirements for the Order Placement Process

Element description	Requirements
Order placement process	• Not more than four process steps • Average order placement cycle time of 120 seconds with an upper specification limit of 180 seconds
Order processing system/ database	• Not more than 30% capacity used for historical data • Transaction rate > 5 transactions/second • Response time < 5 seconds • Network throughput > 500 Kbps
Fax, phone network, and IVR hardware	• Ability to handle up to 100 agents • Skill-based routing with up to twenty skill codes • Automatic call distributor (ACD) handling up to ten voice/fax calls in queue • Router speed of 0.36 seconds/ package
Application server capacity	• One server • Maximum bandwidth of 2×10^{12} bytes/hour • Capacity of 12,000 requests/ hour • Three transactions per minute

4.3 Develop the High-Level Design

The high-level design is a combination of prototypes and designs on paper that are developed to a level of detail where it is possible to predict and test the performance and feasibility of the design.

To develop the high-level design:

1. **Reconfigure the design team.**
2. **Develop the design.**

4.3.1 Reconfigure the design team

1. **Divide or partition the design.**

    • Common methods to divide or partition the design include *intrinsic partitioning* and *extrinsic partitioning.* Intrinsic partitioning (i.e., internal to the design) divides the design tasks so that similar parts of the design are designed together. It is more efficient than extrinsic partitioning, but is more difficult to do. Extrinsic partitioning (i.e., external to the design) separates the design tasks by convenience (e.g., partitioning by customer segment, technology, or geography). It is easier than intrinsic partitioning but can result in overlap and duplicated work if you do not adequately coordinate the activities of any necessary sub-teams.

2. **Determine if sub-teams are appropriate.**

    • As you develop the design, you may be able to split the design tasks among several sub-teams, particularly if the project is large and complex. (For example, a new aircraft design might have sub-teams for the major components [wings, tail, cockpit, etc.] and "sub-sub-teams" within, focusing on designing the electrical, mechanical, ergonomic, and process elements of each component.)

    Choose someone from the "core" design team to lead each sub-team, but staff the teams themselves with subject matter experts. Divide the teams by design element category and give the core design team the coordination responsibilities for the entire project.

For each sub-team, decide:

- How to manage the sub-teams.
- What people resources are needed.
- Where the resources will come from.
- Whether the resources should be full time or part time.
- Which sub-teams will be responsible for which design tasks.

3. **Include all affected managers and project team leaders in staffing discussions.**

- Staffing the sub-teams will require discussion and negotiation among all affected functional managers and project team leaders because:

  - The organization will need to meet both functional and project objectives simultaneously, which may require the same resources. Managers and team leaders may need to negotiate the allocation of these resources.

  - Implementation of the new design will require support from the functional managers. Involving these managers as early as possible in the activities that affect them will help them develop a positive attitude toward the project.

4. **Create charters for the sub-teams.**

- Create charters similar to the overall project charter to allow the sub-teams to work efficiently and effectively. Include:

  - A purpose.
  - A schedule and deadlines.
  - The scope or boundaries for each sub-team's part of the design.

- A description of each team member's responsibilities and functions.

- A clear relationship with the core design team.

- Communication and coordination mechanisms.

5. **Decide if you will use vertical management or horizontal management to coordinate the work of the sub-teams.**

   • Use vertical management to create a hierarchy of sub-teams from higher to lower level. Vertical management ensures that the design tasks at the lower levels are well-integrated and support the common direction set by the higher level tasks. The lower level teams will work on the same design tasks as higher level teams, but at different levels of detail. The higher level sub-teams will meet once or twice a month to set the direction for the project work and then pass this direction on to the lower level sub-teams to complete the design. The lower level sub-teams will meet often (once or twice a week) to communicate and compare notes. They will pass a single, integrated solution on to the higher level teams, who will then determine the next set of design tasks for the lower level teams.

   • Use horizontal management to ensure that diverse parts of the design are integrated, and that the overall design is proceeding according to plan. Sharing best practices across complementary parts of the design ensures that rework and errors are minimized and that the best efforts of every sub-team are freely available to all other sub-team members.

   One or more high-level sub-teams will coordinate horizontal management in meetings once or twice a month. One person (usually the team leader) from each lower level team or set of teams will attend these meetings to synchronize the timelines and share best practices among the teams involved in complementary but non-overlapping parts of the design.

4.3.2 Develop the design

1. **Complete the design of all of the supporting elements defined earlier.**

   • Develop a description of each design element to meet the design requirements. Your final high-level design should include the following elements and deliverables:

Element	Deliverables
Product	• Descriptions and drawings • Legal and regulatory impacts • Models and prototypes • Specifications
Process	• Process flowcharts • Process deployment maps
Information systems	• A logic design • A physical design • A hardware design • Test plan/software scripts • A data migration plan • Test and production equipment • A description of the facilities needed
Human systems	• Job/task analysis • Ergonomic analysis • A training design • Reward and recognition plans • An organizational design • Employee development plans
Equipment	• Descriptions and drawings • Specifications
Materials/ supplies	• A bill of materials • Forms designs • Purchasing and inventory impacts
Facilities	• Architectural drawings • Scale models • Computer models • Layout diagrams

Tip You can develop designs bottom-up, top-down, or in combination. In practice, it is generally preferable to determine the requirements top-down but develop the design bottom-up to ensure that you have included all of the critical elements in your design.

Tip Use common design principles as guidelines to help you produce a higher quality, simpler design. Some common design principles to consider include:

- Never carry out a design without reference to the selected concept.
- Consider the interactions between the various areas of your design.
- Ask if there is a simpler way to accomplish a function.
- Determine if you can eliminate an element altogether.
- Ask if any parts of the design can cover multiple functions.
- Determine if you can combine sections of the design.
- Ask if you can assemble the design from standard parts.
- Outsource tasks or processes that are not core competencies.
- Minimize the number of different people that interact with the customer.
- Consider relocating work to/from the customer.
- Make decisions early in the process to improve efficiency.
- Make decisions late in the process to improve flexibility.

- Minimize handoffs and non-value-added activities.
- Maximize the percentage of value-added time per elapsed time.

• When making design decisions, consider:
  - The required performance range.
  - Environmental conditions.
  - The shelf-life of the process, product, or service.
  - Its reliability under stress.
  - The ease of maintenance.
  - Cost.
  - Safety.
  - Aesthetics.
  - Ergonomics.
  - The ease of standardization or conformance to published standards.

Consideration of these factors will help you as you select design alternatives. Gather information about these factors from subject matter experts, benchmarking data, market research, product knowledge, and business requirements.

The high-level design for the process, human systems, and information systems elements for our order placement process design could include the following four graphics:

A Process Map
(the Process Element)

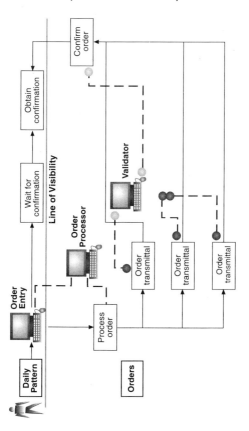

Agent Job Requirements
(the Human Systems Element)

Requirements	Descriptions
Leadership	• Takes initiative and positively influences others to get things done • Willingly embraces and promotes change
Teamwork	• Collaborates and/or coordinates with others to ensure the job gets done • Actively participates on assigned teams • Balances team and individual goal accomplishment and recognition
Customer focus (internal and external)	• Actively listens to the customer, seeks input from customers, and maintains professional demeanor at all times • Identifies the appropriate customer with whom to work • Proactively meets customer needs and follows through on customer/consumer commitments in a timely manner
Decision making	• Makes fact-based decisions in a timely manner
Interpersonal and communication skills	• Actively listens and checks to ensure intended meaning is understood • Communicates clearly, directly, and honestly, both verbally and in writing
Job knowledge	• Thoroughly knows all menus and screens of the desktop and is able to use them effectively • Knows the screens of the order entry system and is able to guide customers through the system • Is able to access status screens of the order processing system and provide confirmation • Has excellent telephone skills

An Architecture Map
(an Information Systems Element)

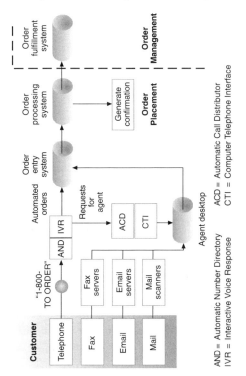

AND = Automatic Number Directory
IVR = Interactive Voice Response

ACD = Automatic Call Distributor
CTI = Computer Telephone Interface

An Application Server Hardware Design
(an Information Systems Element)

Purchase IVR hardware with the following requirements:

- An open, scalable, standards-based framework that forms a unified foundation for customer interaction and enables the real-time integration of diverse media types (including phone, fax, email, and the web) with the ability to accommodate emerging interaction mediums in the future
- A broad suite of call center applications, including inbound and outbound communications routing and reporting, that sit on top of the framework

4.4 Test the High-Level Design

Typically, a high-level design is tested as an integration of all of the elements to ensure that it meets the CTQs. Testing at this stage will also help to identify where pieces of the design do not align and will allow you to correct any problems before attempting a detailed design.

As you test the high-level design, you will determine how the performance of the overall design is affected by the performance of the parts, and how the performance of the output is affected by variability in the inputs.

How do I do it?
1. **Predict the performance of the design.**
2. **Review the high-level design.**

4.4.1 Predict the performance of the design

Because you do not have an operational process, product, or service yet, you cannot test the actual design. Rather, you must make assumptions about the expected performance of the combined design elements that you have developed and check to see if the overall predicted design performance will meet the CTQs, based on these assumptions.

©2004 GOAL/QPC

Clearly, a decision to move forward carries a risk; however, if the assumptions are carefully thought out, the risks associated with this approach are less than the risks associated with building the product or service with no tests at all.

To predict the high-level design performance:

1. **Estimate the performance (mean and variability) of each part of the design.**

2. **Use Simulation to aggregate the performance of the parts and/or Prototyping to test a smaller working verision of the design, to predict the mean and variability of the overall performance. You can also use a Design Scorecard to aggregate sigma scores and predict design performance, especially for product designs.**

What is it?

Simulation allows you to draw conclusions about the behavior of a real or proposed process, product, or service by studying the characteristics of a model. Simulation models help you evaluate the trade-offs between performance and resource requirements to determine an "optimal" design.

Why use it?

- To predict performance when the design is complex or when the risk of failure is high
- To easily change the design or perform "what-if" analysis
- To provide instant feedback of results

- To eliminate the risk of injury or environmental damage

- To reduce raw material or production labor waste

How do I do it?

1. **Specify the problem or questions you wish to test.**

   - Ask:

     - What am I trying to do or predict?

     - What output variable am I trying to measure?

2. **Build a model.**

   - Define the model inputs:

     - Use process flowcharts.

     - Describe the performance in terms of average and variability.

     - Describe the capacity (i.e., the number of resources for each step, volume descriptions, or schedules and shift information).

   - Define the model outputs, including the mean and standard deviation of the overall performance and any other performance metrics specified by the CTQs.

3. **Quantify the model.**

   - Use data from historical records and interviews with subject matter experts.

   - Observe a similar process, product, or service.

   - Use known physical relationships or engineering calculations.

   - Consider using DOE.

4. **Verify and validate the model.**

---

5. Plan and run model scenarios.

- Use the model scenarios to aggregate the performance of the parts to predict the mean and variability of the overall performance.

6. Analyze the results and draw conclusions.

- Compare the average predicted performance with the CTQ performance targets and compare the variability in performance with the CTQ specifications.

7. Make recommendations for adjusting the design.

- Redesign the product or service as necessary and test again.

A Simulation for our multichannel order placement process example could show:

Input: A change in the order arrival rate from 20/hour to 60/hour

Output: The mean and standard deviation of the order placement cycle time

Arrival rate (orders/hour)	Average order placement time (minutes)	Standard deviation of order placement time	Process performance
20	12.28	0.11	Greater than 6 sigma
24	12.70	0.11	Greater than 6 sigma
30	14.39	0.11	Between 5 and 6 sigma
60	105.21	26.75	Failure

In this example, the relationship between performance and volume for a fixed capacity is steeply nonlinear after a certain volume level. As a result, while the process performance drops slowly between an arrival rate of twenty orders per hour and thirty orders per hour, the process fails by the time arrival rates of sixty orders per hour are reached. Therefore, the order placement time is very sensitive to an arrival rate above thirty orders per hour.

Recommendations for adjusting the design could include:

- Identifying the days in the year when the order volume is high.

- Ensuring that extra capacity is available on these days.

- Having a contingency plan for adding capacity quickly if needed.

If it is highly probable that the order volume will exceed sixty orders per hour once or twice a day, then the design is inadequate and redesign and retesting is necessary. But if order volume rarely goes above thirty orders per hour, a contingency plan for adding extra capacity might be sufficient.

What is it?

Prototyping creates a smaller working version of the process, product, or service to allow you to test the design.

Why use it?

- To test one or more elements of the design in greater detail
- To manage risk and uncertainty (particularly for high-risk components or subsystems of the design)

How do I do it?

1. **Identify the highly focused specific questions or limited number of technical issues you want to investigate.**

2. **Determine the key interfaces (e.g., customer to component, critical component to critical component, etc.) that you want to focus on.**

3. **Select a prototype.**
   - Use something that already exists to test the concept (i.e., modify an existing product or repackage a competitor's product) or simulate the end product without providing the actual product itself (i.e., create components that look and feel like the end product or put components together to simulate the product's end function).

4. **Test the prototype.**

What is it?

The Design Scorecard allows you to collect, display, and analyze the facts of a product design to predict future performance and improve upon the initial design. The scorecard compares the customer CTQs to the predicted performance of the design elements to see how the design is progressing.

A typical Design Scorecard includes five component scorecards: the performance sigma scorecard, the parts sigma scorecard, the process sigma scorecard, the software sigma scorecard, and the top-level scorecard (which is a summary of the other four scorecards). (Note: The specific component scorecards you use may vary with the product you are designing [e.g., you might not need a software sigma scorecard if no software is involved in the design], but the scorecard generation would be similar.) You can categorize the data entered into each of the component scorecards under four main headings: CTQ/parameter details, the Voice of the Customer, the Voice of the Product, and performance metrics.

Why use it?

- To predict performance, using a statistical model

- To optimize a design

- To recognize missing key elements or issues in a design

- To locate areas in the design that need improvement

- To communicate with all stakeholders

- To record design progress and store lessons learned

  Note: The primary purpose of the Design Scorecard is to encourage and support a dialogue within the design team. The questions the team asks when using the scorecard are more powerful than using the scorecard to drive toward a set answer

---

or sigma score. (Ultimately, it will be the customer or end user who will determine whether the design is satisfactory, not the scores on a scorecard.)

As you discuss the Design Scorecards, ask the following questions to initiate a dialogue about your design:

- What are the customer expectations?
- What are the capabilities of the parts, process, and product?
- What is the current Voice of the Process (i.e., the information about how all of the process variables within a process and the process itself are performing)?
- How can we create a robust design?
- Have we included all parties and processes?
- Are there any gaps between reality and prediction?
- What are the intended consequences? Unintended consequences?
- Can this success be replicated?

Note: An in-depth discussion of the Design Scorecard is beyond the scope of this book. For additional information, see *Design for Six Sigma: A Roadmap for Product Development* by Kai Yang and Basem S. El-Haik, McGraw-Hill, 2003.

How do I do it?

1. Create a performance sigma scorecard.

- Include all of the important product performance parameters. Use statistical estimates to measure the effect that component variation will have on product performance and to measure product behavior against customer specifications.

Tip Use either attribute defects per unit (DPU) or variable data in the calculations for the performance sigma scorecard. The data you use in this scorecard can come from FMEA analysis, benchmarking, QFD Matrices, test designs, Simulations and analysis, product test data and results, customer complaints and audit results, and contracts and warranty issues.

a) Determine the performance parameter details.

- List all critical performance parameters (or CTQs) associated with the product.
- Assign metrics and units to each of the critical performance parameters.

b) Record the Voice of the Customer data.

- For parameters measured using variable data, obtain a target and specification limits. (Note: The specification limits might be one-sided.)
- For parameters measured using attribute data, obtain the target defect level (usually 0).

c) Record the Voice of the Product data.

- Denote the data collected as either long-term (LT) data or short-term (ST) data.
- Enter the observed mean and standard deviation or parts per million (PPM) defects for the measured performance parameters.

d) Record the performance metrics.

- Calculate the sigma value for the upper specification limit (Z USL), the sigma value for the lower specification limit (Z LSL), and the defects per unit (DPU) for each performance parameter.
- Calculate the rolled throughput yield (RTY) for each performance parameter, using the equation:

$$RTY = e^{-DPU}$$

(**Note**: An in-depth discussion of sigma values and rolled throughput yield is beyond the scope of this book. For more information, see *The Black Belt Memory Jogger*™.)

Tip All DPU and RTY calculations should be based on long-term data. If you are using short-term data, you will need to approximate long-term DPU by assuming the relationship:

$$Z_{ST} = Z_{LT} + 1.5$$

(Note: This relationship is true for both Z USL and Z LSL [i.e., Z USL$_{ST}$ = Z USL $_{LT}$ + 1.5, and Z LSL$_{ST}$ = Z LSL $_{LT}$ + 1.5].)

- Calculate the total DPU for performance as the sum of the individual performance parameter DPUs. Then calculate the overall performance using the equation:

$$RTY = e^{-\text{total DPU}}$$

e) Interpret the information compiled in the performance sigma scorecard by asking:

- Is our yield or sigma value competitive?

- What are the drivers for this performance?

- Which parameters perform best? Which parameters perform worst?

- How critical are these parameters for our customers?

- Are any design trade-offs possible to improve performance?

- Are our measurement systems adequate?

- What are our model assumptions? Are they valid?

- How can I make a cost-based analysis?

Design 189

Note: This discussion of the scorecard results will often lead to an improved version of the design and more-robust product performance.

The Performance Sigma Scorecard for a Treadmill

Parameter	Metric unit	Data type	Target	USL	LSL	LT/ST	Mean	Std. dev.	Z USL	Z LSL	DPU	RTY
Quietness	sone	Variable	0	1.2		ST	0.8	0.15	1.17	N/A	1.21E-01	0.88603
Speed change	mi.	Variable	0.1	0.2	0.05	LT	0.1	0.06	1.67	0.83	2.50E-01	0.77871
Reliability	mi.	Variable	500		300	LT	350	30	N/A	1.67	4.78E-02	0.95333
Safety	no. of problems	Attribute	0			LT					1.00E-02	0.99005
										Total	4.29E-01	0.65122

Total number of parameters	4
Avg. defect per parameter	0.1072
Avg. yield per parameter	0.8983
Avg. parameter LT sigma	1.2720
Avg. parameter ST sigma	2.7720

Tip Use the information within the performance sigma scorecard to:

- Determine how robust the design is, subject to normal variation.
- Estimate the defects that the customer will experience.
- Determine if the defects are mainly due to design, reliability, or performance issues.
- Combine various CTQ levels into a single score for comparison.

When creating and using this scorecard:

- Start from the customer perspective.
- Identify and prioritize all of the customer CTQs.
  - Do not omit critical customer requirements.
- Translate the requirements into technical data.
  - Remember that variable data requires fewer samples than attribute data.
  - Make sure you have the most appropriate measure for the requirements.
- Perform measurement system analysis on the key metrics (i.e., make sure that the measurement system you are using to measure key metrics is reliable and accurate).
- Be aware of unexpressed assumptions (e.g., normality, units, etc.).
- Verify that the data represents long-term variation, and if the data is not normally distributed, transform it.
- Do not get caught up in unwarranted minutiae.

---

2. Create a parts sigma scorecard.

- Calculate the sigma scores (capability metrics) for the parts, sub-assemblies, and final assemblies used in the product. Use statistical estimates to determine the defect levels of incoming parts in terms of DPMO and PPM. (Include a parts list with defect-data-by-part to help you evaluate and choose high-quality suppliers.)

  - Combine the defect levels from all critical parts for a total score.

  Note: Use incoming inspection data, past experiences, similar parts, purchasing department data, supplier data, and external agencies' data as your sources of information for this scorecard.

a) Record the part CTQ details.

  - List the relevant part descriptors (e.g., supplier, part number, part name, etc.) for each part being measured.

  - List the quantity of parts per assembly or sub-assembly and sum to find the total number of parts used.

  - Assign metrics and units to each of the parts being measured.

b) Record the Voice of the Customer data.

  - For each part measured using variable data, obtain a target and specification limits. (Note: The specification limits might be one-sided.)

  - For parts measured using attribute data, obtain the target defect level (usually 0).

---

c) Record the Voice of the Product data.

- Denote the data collected as either LT or ST data.
- Enter the observed mean and standard deviation or PPM defects for the measured parts.

d) Record the performance metrics.

- Calculate Z USL, Z LSL, and DPU for each part.
- Calculate the RTY for each part, using the equation:

$$RTY = e^{-DPU}$$

- Calculate the total DPU for parts as the sum of the individual part DPUs. Then calculate the overall part RTY using the equation:

$$RTY = e^{-\text{total DPU}}$$

e) Interpret the information compiled in the parts sigma scorecard by asking:

- What are the drivers for the current level of parts scores?
- Which parts are of the best quality? Worst quality?
- Would an alternate supplier improve the scores?
- What are the cost considerations?
- Is there a way to reduce the number of parts (e.g., adjusting the design so that some parts are not needed)?
- What are the possible trade-offs to improve?
- Are our measurement systems adequate?
- What are our model assumptions? Are they valid?

The Parts Sigma Scorecard for a Treadmill

Major part assembly	Major part no.	Minor part assembly	Supplier	Parameter	Metric unit	Data type	Target	USL	LSL	LT/ST	Mean	Std. dev.	Z USL	Z LSL	DPU	RTY
Base assembly	CL006	Hframe	Gfab	Length	in.	Variable	43	43.2	42.8	LT	42.95	0.05	5.00	3.00	1.35E-03	0.998651
				Breadth	in.	Variable	13	13.2	12.8	LT	13.02	0.05	3.60	4.40	1.65E-04	0.999835
		Pulleys	Gfab	Thickness	in.	Variable	0.27	0.3	0.24	LT	0.27	0.0102	2.90	2.98	3.29E-03	0.996712
				Tension	lbs.	Variable	8	14	2	LT	8	1.81	3.314917	3.314917	9.17E-04	0.999084
				Width	in.	Variable	0.25	0.3	0.2	LT	0.255	0.0152	2.960526	3.618421	1.68E-03	0.998318
Base stabilizer	MA003	Adjustment Bracket	FlyByCo	Adjustment level	pass/fail	Attribute	pass			LT					2.43E-04	0.999757
		Wheel Stop	FlyByCo	In position	in/out	Attribute	in			LT					1.56E-04	0.999844
														Total	7.81E-03	0.992222

Note: This is a truncated version of a parts scorecard, which would include all of the parts and be more extensive.

Tip Use the information within the parts sigma scorecard to:

- Determine the quality level of key parts used in the design.
- Track the incoming defect levels of critical supplier parts.
- Improve communication among stakeholders.

When creating and using this scorecard:

- Include only the parts and assemblies that impact the CTQs.
- Use a good classification system for assemblies and sub-assemblies.
- Remember that variable data requires fewer samples than attribute data.
- Perform measurement system analysis on the key metrics.
- Do not omit CTQ parts.
- Be aware of unexpressed assumptions (e.g., normality, units, etc.).
- Verify that the data represents long-term variation. If data is not normally distributed, transform it.
- Do not get caught up in unwarranted minutiae.

3. **Create a process sigma scorecard.**

- Include sigma scores for all of the processes for building sub-assemblies and final assemblies (based on detailed process maps), and calculate the process capability to help you identify process improvement opportunities. Use statistical estimates to determine the defect levels of processes (measured in terms of parts, assemblies, and final product) and to measure the process behavior (i.e., the Voice of the Process, measured against process specifications).

Tip Use the following information as sources of information for this scorecard:

- Top-level and detailed process maps and flowcharts, with process capability data from models, Simulations, and workflow analyses

- Manufacturing design documents and specifications (from engineering departments) (Note: Include details on process data and assumptions from standard operating procedures and major component plans)

- CTQ process data for Critical to the Process parameters (Note: Include process prioritization tools, data from measurement systems and inspection points, and process capability data from existing quality systems)

- Manufacturing process database and past process records (Note: Include performance indicators for labor and material utilization, financial data, and outgoing defect data)

- Incoming defects.

a) Record the process step CTQ details.

- List the major and critical process steps for the final assembly.
- List the requirements/CTQs for each of the process steps.
- Assign metrics and units to each of the process step CTQs.

b) Record the Voice of the Customer data.

- For process step CTQs measured using variable data, obtain a target and specification limits. (Note: The specification limits might be one-sided.)
- For process step CTQs measured using attribute data, obtain the target defect level (usually 0).

---

c) Record the Voice of the Product data.

- Denote the data collected as either LT or ST data.

- Enter the observed mean and standard deviation or PPM defects for the measured process step.

d) Record the performance metrics.

- Calculate Z USL, Z LSL, and DPU for each process step.

- Calculate the RTY for each process step, using the equation:

$$RTY = e^{-DPU}$$

- Calculate the total DPU for the process as the sum of the individual process step DPUs. Then calculate the overall process RTY using the equation:

$$RTY = e^{-total\ DPU}$$

e) Interpret the information in the process sigma scorecard by asking:

- Does our measurement system allow us to analyze all critical processes adequately?

- What are the drivers for the current process performance scores?

- What are the possible trade-offs to improve current performance?

- How does the process sigma scorecard compare with the parts sigma scorecard?

- Does the process sigma scorecard reflect the performance sigma scorecard results?

- Are parts and processes interacting to produce a high number of defects?

- Are our process sequencing assumptions valid?

- Are the processes different? Which processes are best? Worst?

The Process Sigma Scorecard for a Treadmill

Process steps for final assembly	Parameter	Metric unit	Data type	Target	USL	LSL	LT/ST	Mean	Std. dev.	Z USL	Z LSL	DPU	RTY
Attach motor to base	Tension	lbs.	Variable	8	8.5	7.5	LT	7.9	0.15	4.00	2.67	3.86E-03	100%
Attach console column	Height	in.	Variable	34	34.2	33.8	LT	34	0.08	2.50	2.50	1.24E-02	99%
Attach motor housing	Gaps	yes/no	Attribute	0			LT					1.00E-03	100%
Attach handle bars	Visual	yes/no	Attribute	0			LT					1.00E-02	99%
											Total	2.73E-02	0.9731

Note: This is a truncated version of a process scorecard, showing only the major process steps for the final assembly. All of the process steps in the manufacture and assembly of the product would be included in the full version.

Tip Use the information in the process sigma scorecard to:

• Determine the current quality levels of the critical processes.

• Estimate the effect of the design on manufacturing process performance.

• Analyze the required quality levels to realize product performance.

• Enhance data-driven communication among all stakeholders.

• Encourage design-for-manufacturability principles by bridging manufacturing and engineering.

• Combine various CTQ processes into a single score for comparison.

When using the process sigma scorecard:

• Use only critical processes prioritized using the QFD Matrix, Cause & Effect Matrix, and FMEA.

• Have top-level and detailed process maps for critical processes that include (at a minimum) specifications, current defect levels, product volume, labor and material requirements, and costing information.

• Remember that variable data requires fewer samples than attribute data.

• Perform measurement system analysis on the key metrics.

• When in doubt, consider the next process as the customer.

• Be aware of assumptions about the number of defect opportunities.

4. Create a software sigma scorecard.

• Include all of the steps in the software development process and compute the efficiency in each phase, to help eliminate defects in each stage of development.

a) Record the software CTQ details.

- List the software development process phases.
- List the requirements for each phase.
- Assign metrics and units to each of the software requirements.

b) Record the Voice of the Customer data.

- For software requirement CTQs measured using variable data, obtain a target and specification limits. (Note: The specification limits might be one-sided.)
- For software requirement CTQs measured using attribute data, obtain the target defect level (usually 0).

c) Record the Voice of the Product data.

- Denote the data collected as either LT or ST data.
- Enter the observed mean and standard deviation or PPM defects for the measured software requirements.

d) Record the performance metrics.

- Calculate the Z USL, Z LSL, and DPU for each software requirement.
- Calculate the RTY for each requirement, using the equation:
$$RTY = e^{-DPU}$$
- Calculate the total DPU for software as the sum of the individual requirement DPUs. Then calculate the overall software RTY using the equation:
$$RTY = e^{-\text{total DPU}}$$

The Software Sigma Scorecard for a Treadmill

Software development phase for tread-mill console assembly	Parameter	Metric unit	Data type	Target	USL	LSL	LT/ST	Mean	Std. dev.	Z USL	Z LSL	DPU	RTY
Requirements	Completeness	no. of incomplete	Attribute	0			LT					0.04	0.960789
Top design	Accuracy	no. of errors	Attribute	0			LT					0.03	0.970446
Program logic	Accuracy	no. of errors	Attribute	0			LT					0.012	0.988072
Data definitions	Accuracy	no. of errors	Attribute	0			LT					0.065	0.937067
Hardware interface	Compatibility	yes/ no	Attribute	yes			LT					0.016	0.984127
System test	Success	pass/ fail	Attribute	pass			LT					0.16	0.852144
Packaging	Accuracy	yes/ no	Attribute	yes			LT					0.08	0.923116
Documentation	Completeness	yes/ no	Attribute	yes			LT					0.4	0.67032
											Total	0.803	0.447983

Tip Develop the software sigma score estimates by:

- Using either attribute DPU or variable data.
- Selecting key metrics at each phase and computing defects (e.g., time to debug, number of reworks, design review attendance, etc.).
- Calculating the probability of software defects at each phase, based on historical data.
- Summarizing the DPMO for each software module and the overall DPMO.

Use information within this scorecard to:

- Determine the reliability of critical software components.
- Track defects in each major step of each software development phase.
- Compute your efficiency to detect and eliminate defects in each phase.
- Analyze the required quality levels to realize the cost-effectiveness and timeliness of the software development cycles.
- Encourage design-for-manufacturability principles by bridging design and delivery teams.
- Combine various CTQ processes into a single score for comparison.

When using the software sigma scorecard:

- Make sure that the scorecard contains all of the critical steps of the software development phases.
- Prioritize and apply the scorecard in critical areas first.
- Catch errors early and fix them as soon as possible. (The rework cost to fix an error at a later stage increases geometrically.)

- Include Software Engineering Institute (SEI) assessments (instead of defects per line of code), historical databases of defects, manuals, and defects data from field error logs and logs of customer calls, as good sources of information.

Tip When developing software:

- Adopt an efficient software development methodology.
- Do not hesitate to apply the design process to the software development process.
- Follow the SEI Capability Maturity Model (CMM) and operate at CMM Level 3 and above.

5. **Develop the top-level scorecard.**

   a) Input the total DPU values obtained from each of the individual component scorecards.

   b) Calculate total product DPU as the sum of the component scorecard DPUs.

   c) Input the component scorecard sigma values and calculate the overall product design sigma value (using the information from the component scorecards and standard process sigma calculations).

Note: If you have generated multiple scorecards for various product assembly levels for the performance, parts, processes, and software, you can summarize the overall DPU and sigma levels in the top-level scorecard by including the total DPU from each scorecard you generated. Alternatively, you can generate an "intermediate-level component scorecard" that summarizes the information from the various product assembly levels for each of the four components and then subsequently summarize this intermediate-level information in the top-level product scorecard.

The Top-Level Sigma Scorecard for a Treadmill

Top-Level Scorecard

Treadmill	Performance		Parts		Process		Software		Product Capability	
	DPU	no. of opp.	DPU	no. of opp.	DPU	no. of opp.	DPU	no. of opp.	DPU	no. of opp.
Top level	0.429	4	0.0242	8	0.0373	5	142	3020	143.67	3046
Base assembly	0.959	1	0.0116	4	0.2138	4				
Totals	1.388	5	0.0358	12	0.2511	9	142	3020	143.67	
RTY	0.24957		0.96483		0.778		2.1E-62		4E-63	
Z LT	-0.6758		1.80976		0.7653		-5E+06		-5E-06	
DPU/opp	0.2776		0.00298		0.0279		0.04702		0.0472	
RTY	0.7576		0.99702		0.9725		0.95407		0.9539	
Sigma/Opp (Z LT)	0.6986		2.75009		1.9187		1.68565		1.6842	LT Sigma
Sigma/Opp (Z ST)	2.1986		4.25009		3.4187		3.18565		3.1842	ST Sigma

Tip Use the top-level scorecard to:

- Collect performance, parts, process, and software sigma scores in a single place to help locate problem areas.
- Determine the quality levels of the critical design elements.
- Estimate the defects you expect to find during transitions.
- Realize product performance by analyzing the required quality levels.
- Enhance data-driven communication among all stakeholders.
- Encourage design-for-manufacturability principles by bridging manufacturing, engineering, marketing, and information systems.

When evaluating the top-level scorecard:

- Start from the customer perspective.
- Consider cost in all design decisions.
- Include all processes, parts, and parameters that are critical customer requirements.
- Review the scorecard in standard design reviews.
- Use the scorecard system as a tool for improving the design, not as a grading system.
- Use DPUs (rather than sigma scores) to better understand a situation. (Sigma scores can mask issues.)
- Do not let the scorecard replace sound engineering and business judgment; use the scorecard to supplement existing tools.

Note: You may need to change some elements of the high-level design based on the Simulation, Prototyping, or Design Scorecard results. The results may require you to generate and test several alternatives by rerunning the Simulations or by building prototypes and retesting them.

When the Simulation, Prototyping, and/or Design Scorecard results indicate that the predicted design will meet the CTQs, document the final high-level design and complete all of the high-level design requirements.

Perform cost assessments to ensure that the cost of the design is within the acceptable range. Ensure that the risks associated with the design are identified and that risk management plans are developed as appropriate. "Freeze" the design requirements and conduct the high-level design review.

4.4.2 Review the high-level design

1. **Conduct a technical review of the high-level design.**

   • Evaluate the completeness and accuracy of the capability testing results to ensure that the design will meet the CTQs.

   • Identify critical areas of risk and actions to mitigate that risk.

   • Ensure that regulatory and legal requirements are satisfied.

2. **Conduct an organizational review of the high-level design.**

   • Identify and discuss any project management issues for the upcoming detailed design.

Note: Unlike the concept review, the high-level design review usually does not involve customers.

3. **Conduct a high-level tollgate review.**

   • Focus on:

     - The prioritized high-level design requirements.

     - Any designs on paper of the key elements.

     - Results from Simulation, Prototyping, and/or the Design Scorecard.

     - The cost/benefit analysis results.

     - The identification of high-risk areas and risk management plans.

The outputs of the high-level design review will include:

   • A list of risk factors and action items, with owners and time frames identified.

   • A list of additional analyses to be performed, if any.

   • Dates for future high-level design reviews, if needed.

   • A project plan for the detailed design.

This review can lead you to:

   • Check the input data for prediction.

   • Revisit the concept to see if changes are needed.

   • Revisit the Multistage Plan and adjust what will go into each phase.

   • Move to detailed design.

4.5 Identify and Prioritize the Detailed Design Elements

The process to identify and prioritize the detailed design elements is similar to the process for the high-level design elements, but is at a greater level of detail. Use the same element categories that you did for the high-level design (i.e., products/service elements, information systems elements, human systems elements, etc.) but design them to the next level of detail.

> **Tip** As you move from high-level design to detailed design, be careful not to make the creative system-level decisions at the detailed design stage that you made in the concept or high-level design stage; instead, make very specific decisions on the design elements that you already selected. Understand how these decisions fit together and how to manage the project to allow the diverse parts of the design to come together at the right time and at the right cost.

How do I do it?

1. **Identify the detailed design elements.**

   • Define the high-level design elements to the next level of detail, to identify the specific elements and requirements for the detailed design. Choose:

   - The specific vendors, programs, hardware products, training packages, hiring agencies, etc., that you will need to complete the design development.

   - The process and input variables (process control variables) that you will measure and monitor to ensure that the service performance is under control.

For example, the detailed design equipment category for our order placement process might include:

Element descript.	High-level design	High-level requirements	Detailed design
IVR hardware	• An open, scalable, standards-based framework that forms a unified foundation for customer interaction and enables the real-time integration of diverse media types, including phone, fax, email, and the web, with the ability to accommodate emerging interaction mediums in the future • A broad suite of call center applications including inbound and outbound communications routing and reporting that sit on top of the framework	• Able to handle up to 100 agents • Skill-based routing with up to twenty skill codes • ACD handling up to ten voice/fax calls in queue • Router speed of 0.36 seconds/package	Supported third-party applications: • Enterprise Resource Planning (ERP Resource Suite) • Customer Information Systems (Inforsyst, Inc.) • Sales Force Automation (Inforsyst, Inc.) • Performance Monitoring (pmdsystems .com) Supported network operating systems: • Computernet Cosmos • Webnetport IV Switch: • Pakin Hicomm • ATPS 6FQ13 • Belmont 1000 Supported desktop integration standards: Port Collector 9, Wildcat, Ultra-deck EQ

2. **Determine which detailed design elements and process control variables are most important.**

   • The most important detailed design elements are those that impact the most important high-level design elements. The most important process control variables are those that should be monitored carefully because they are usually the leading indicators of deteriorating process performance.

• Create a QFD Matrix (QFD 4) with the high-level design elements in the rows and the detailed design elements and/or process control variables in the columns. (Note: For product designs, you may need to create a separate QFD Matrix for each high-level design element because of the many components for each high-level element.) For each element/function relationship, ask, "To what extent does this detailed element impact the performance of this high-level element?" Use the 9, 3, 1 scale and matrix multiplication to help you prioritize the elements.

Note: It is also appropriate to enter the high-level design *requirements* in the rows of the matrix. Typically, at this stage, the decisions to choose specific pieces of software or hardware are based upon the requirements (i.e., to what extent does the selected product meet the requirements for the design).

Tip For designs that you will develop yourself, the importance ratings of the detailed design elements help to show where you should spend the most time in development. For designs that use commercial software or hardware purchased from a third party, the importance ratings help to determine where to place the greatest effort in evaluation and where to focus your integration efforts.

Prioritizing the detailed design elements for our order placement process could result in the following QFD Matrix:

QFD Matrix for the Detailed Design Elements

High-Level Design Elements	Phone network hardware X	IVR hardware Y	Order processing system Z	Average order volume/day	Percentage of complex orders	Percentage of customers dropping out of IVR	Percentage of orders with errors	Importance (from QFD 3)
Order placement process					9		9	89
Fax and phone network	9			9				57
IVR hardware/ software		9	9	9			3	52
Order processing system			9	3			3	52
Order processing agents				9	9	9	9	49
How important	113	468	468	1110	1242	491	1398	

Note: Although this QFD Matrix combines the detailed design elements and the process control variables, this combination may not always be possible. You may need to separate the two types of variables, depending on the complexity of the problem.

In this example matrix, the input variables (the percentage of orders with errors, the percentage of complex orders, and the average order volume per day) are more important than the design elements (the hardware or software purchased); it is therefore critical to design a robust process control system.

4.6 Develop the Detailed Design

Note: As you proceed from theoretical design to actual development, the design activities may take quite a bit of time, depending on the complexity of the detailed design process. The actual time necessary will depend on how much development work you need to do.

How do I do it?

1. **Complete the design of all of the supporting elements.**

   • You may use other design methodologies (e.g., standard software design methodologies) to develop the various elements of the design and to provide the details for each element and the associated deliverables.

2. **Ensure that you have included all of the elements of the design and that no gaps remain.**

   • Make sure that all of the necessary aspects of the design have been handed over to sub-teams.

3. **Make sure that the design schedules can accommodate the design and the integration of the various elements.**

4. **Ensure that good communication exists between the design sub-teams.**

   • Communicate frequently to ensure that the design is proceeding smoothly and on schedule.

5. **Use design principles to guide the design process.**

   • Develop specific deliverables for each element category and for the prioritized high-level and detailed design elements. Consider the following principles when addressing each category:

Category	Deliverables	Principles (Consider design features that:)
Product elements	• Descriptions and drawings • Legal and regulatory impacts • Models and prototypes • Specifications	• Transform the product to something better or more desirable • Distinguish the product or service • Create more value to the customer • Make the product or service expandable
Process elements	• Proces flowcharts • Process deployment maps	• Focus on interactions with the customer (i.e., the "moments of truth") • Minimize rework • Minimize or eliminate inefficiencies or non-value-added activities • Minimize inspections • Minimize variability • Minimize hand-offs • Minimize potential errors/failures
Information systems elements	• A logic design • A physical design • A hardware design • Test plan/software scripts • A data migration plan • Test and production environment • A description of the facilities needed	• Obtain current and on-going customer feedback • Make appropriate information accessible at the workplace • Automate the collection, storage, and transfer of information • Clarify what information is needed, when it is needed, where in the process, and by whom • Ensure that there is timely and easy access to the information
Human systems elements	• Job/task analysis • Ergonomic analysis • A training design • Reward and recognition plans • An organizational design	• Organize around work processes • Assign responsibilities for complete processes • Move decision making to the workplace

Continued on next page

Category	Deliverables	Principles (Consider design features that:)
Human systems elements (continued)	• Employee development plans	• Enlarge and enrich jobs • Match jobs with skill levels • Identify and nurture core competencies • Create an environment for intrinsic motivation • Provide an opportunity for career growth
Equipment	• Descriptions and drawings • Specifications	• Minimize fixed investments • Automate routine work • Ensure the reliability and maintainability of necessary equipment
Materials/ supplies	• A bill of materials • Forms designs • Purchasing and inventory impacts	• Minimize inventory • Maximize inventory turnover • Form partnerships with suppliers
Facilities	• Architectural drawings • Scale models • Computer models • Layout diagrams	• Combine centralization and decentralization • Minimize motion and distances traveled • Organize the workspace in the appropriate sequence of the work process • Consider ergonomic issues such as lighting, proper body mechanics, fatigue, morale, and distractions • Prevent injury • Consider person/ machine interactions

Note: These design principles are more specific than the ones used in the high-level design in that they pertain to each element of the design.

4.7 Test the Detailed Design

Because you tested the high-level design before moving on to the detailed design, it is not necessary to test all of the pieces of the design again. Instead, test only those parts of the design that are vulnerable to failure.

To test the vulnerable parts of the design:

1. **Identify the points of vulnerability.**

    • Consider:

      - New or untested technology.

      - Transition points, especially to and from manual processes.

      - Customer "moments of truth."

      - Parts of the design that are susceptible to significant input variability (based on data from the process management system; for new designs that may not have process management systems in place yet, use data from Simulations, research, benchmarking, or technical knowledge).

      - Parts of the design that are susceptible to catastrophic failure (based on the past experience of subject matter experts).

2. **Test the points of vulnerability using Simulation, FMEA/EMEA, and/or Design Scorecards.**

Note: If you uncover performance gaps in this testing, develop potential solutions and repeat the capability testing until you achieve acceptable results. Once the detailed design is tested, use FMEA/EMEA to identify and address any remaining significant risks.

FMEA/
EMEA

What is it?

The Failure Mode and Effects Analysis or Error Mode and Effects Analysis identifies the points in a process where problems might occur, provides a numerical score for these potential problems, and helps you decide which actions to take to avoid such problems.

Note: An FMEA assesses product, component, or system failures. An EMEA assesses processes in which the primary failures are human errors.

Why use it?

- To identify high-risk areas where a process, product, or service might fail
- To help develop action plans to prevent the causes of those failures
- To make a process robust enough so that the causes of potential failures will not affect it

How do I do it?

1. List the steps of a process (or the components of a product if you are creating a product design) in the left-hand column of a matrix.

2. For each process step or component, list potential failure modes or ways in which the process, product, or service might fail.

3. List the potential consequences or effects of each failure (e.g., defective product, wrong information, delays, etc.) in the matrix and rate the severity of each consequence on a scale of 1–10.

   Tip There can be multiple failures for each step and multiple effects for each failure. Score each separately.

4. List the potential causes of the effects and rate their likelihood of occurrence on a scale of 1–10.

5. List the controls that you currently have in place for the process and rate your ability to detect each potential cause on a scale of 1–10.

   Tip Develop your own scales for severity, occurrence, and detection, or use the sample scales shown on the following page.

Sample Severity, Occurrence, and Detection Scales

Severity = Likely impact of the failure

	Rating	Criteria: A failure could . . .
Bad	10	Injure a customer or employee
	9	Be illegal
	8	Render the product or service unfit for use
	7	Cause extreme customer dissatisfaction
	6	Result in partial malfunction
	5	Cause a loss of performance likely to result in a complaint
	4	Cause minor performance loss
	3	Cause a minor nuisance; can be overcome with no loss
	2	Be unnoticed; minor effect on performance
Good	1	Be unnoticed and not affect the performance

Occurrence = How often the cause will occur

	Rating	Time Period	Probability
Bad	10	More than once per day	> 30%
	9	Once every 3–4 days	< 30%
	8	Once per week	< 5%
	7	Once per month	< 1%
	6	Once every 3 months	< .03%
	5	Once every 6 months	< 1 per 10,000
	4	Once per year	< 6 per 100,000
	3	Once every 1–3 years	< 6 per million
	2	Once every 3–6 years	< 3 per 10 million
Good	1	Once every 6–100 years	< 2 per billion

Detection = How likely we are to know if the cause has occurred

	Rating	Definition
Bad	10	Defect caused by failure is not detectable
	9	Occasional units are checked for defects
	8	Units are systematically sampled and inspected
	7	All units are manually inspected
	6	Manual inspection with mistake-proofing modifications
	5	Process is monitored via statistical process control (SPC) and manually inspected
	4	SPC used, with an immediate reaction to out-of-control conditions
	3	SPC as above, with 100% inspection surrounding out-of-control conditions
	2	All units are automatically inspected
Good	1	Defect is obvious and can be kept from affecting customer

6. For each row, determine the risk of each failure mode by multiplying the severity x the occurrence x the detection in the row. Record the result of this calculation as the risk priority number (RPN) in the matrix.

7. Identify recommended actions to reduce or eliminate the risks associated with high RPNs and list the actions in the matrix.

   Tip You can recalculate the RPNs for any failure mode after you determine which action you will take to avoid those failures.

Note: The example on the next page combines failure modes and error modes in a single chart. This type of combination can be appropriate if the risks associated with the two modes are not significantly different and can be compared to each other.

The FMEA analysis in this example is also at a high level of detail. More typically, an FMEA is conducted on just one part of the process, but at a greater level of detail; in such cases, you may need to create a larger, more complete FMEA.

A Sample FMEA/EMEA Chart from the Order Placement Process

Item/ Process Step	Potential Failure Mode	Potential Effect(s) of Failure	Severity	Potential Cause(s) of Failure	Occurrence	Current Controls	Detection	RPN	Recommended Actions
Order entry	Customer cannot place order	Customer is dissatisfied	7	Telephone network is dead	5	Telephone company provides notification	1	35	Current control is adequate
	Customer cannot place order	Customer is dissatisfied	7	Network is overloaded because of unexpected call volume	8	No current controls (process does not exist)	10	560	Monitor average speed of answer automatically; provide warning if above limit
Order processing	Customer's order is not recorded	Customer does not receive ordered item	7	Order recording system is down	6	Periodic system monitoring	8	336	More systematic monitoring
	Customer's order is incompletely or inaccurately recorded	Customer receives wrong items	6	Order entry data is incorrect	9	No current controls	10	540	Introduce passive validity checks as much as possible
Order validation/ confirmation	Order not validated	Customer doesn't have proof that order is complete	5	System is not working	6	Periodic system monitoring	8	240	More systematic monitoring
	Order confirmed in error	Customer is misinformed	6	Communication problems between catalog systems and order entry system	4	No current controls	10	240	To be determined
Order transmission	Order not transmitted	Customer does not receive items	7	System is not working	6	Periodic system monitoring	8	336	More systematic monitoring
	Order transmission hung	Customer does not receive items	7	Communication problem	4	Can be detected	1	28	Current control is adequate

4.8 Develop the Process Management Plans

A process management plan is a well-defined plan of action for monitoring processes in the context of the entire organization. The plan helps to manage the process "end-to-end," focuses on actionable steps and integration with day-to-day management, and helps to ensure that the design will continue to meet the CTQs over time.

The process management plan can also help you collect and analyze data during the pilot. You will use the same framework to collect data during the pilot that you will use to collect data after implementation because the types of data collected and the analyses conducted are the same in both situations.

Note: Obviously, process management plans are necessary when designing a process or service, but you will also need process management plans for product designs, to manage the processes and services that make and support the product.

> **Tip** Your organization may already have a process management approach defined and in use. Use your organization's current process management approach if appropriate.

To develop a process management plan:

1. **Determine the structure and composition of the process management team(s).**

   • Ask:

     - Who are the team members?

     - What functions will they serve on the team?

     - Who are the permanent and rotating members?

     - Who is the team leader?

- How often does the team meet?
- What is the structure of the process management team meetings?

• Include process owners who will be impacted by the implementation of the design project and communicate with them regularly throughout the design process. You may need to include teams of process owners to ensure that the system that supports the new design will continue to operate as expected.

2. **Document the key processes of the process management plan.**

   • Ask:
   - Are all process flows at the appropriate level?
   - Are there clearly articulated links between high-level and low-level documentation?
   - Have methods and procedures been created from low-level flows?
   - Are document control plans in place to change obsolete material?
   - Do the key processes follow corporate documentation standards?

3. **Determine the critical metrics for monitoring performance.**

   • Consider:
   - What key CTQs need to be monitored.
   - What the relationships between the CTQs and critical process and input measures are.
   - If the definitions of all metrics are complete and documented.
   - If the measures focus on both leading and lagging indicators.

- If the measures are actionable and easy to understand.
- If customer satisfaction and employee satisfaction measures have been linked to the CTQs.
- If learning and growth measures are included.

4. **Define the data collection, analysis, and reporting plans.**
   - Ask:
     - How should we collect the data required for reporting?
     - Is any manual data collection needed?
     - How often should we collect the data?
     - What is the sampling plan for data collection?
     - What tools are needed to analyze the data?
     - What display formats will we use?
     - What is the structure and content of the performance reports?
     - Who receives the performance reports and how often?

5. **Create an intervention and process improvement plan.**
   - Ask:
     - What action plans need to be in place to address performance issues?
     - What is the follow-up process to ensure that action plans have been implemented?
     - What are the triggers to initiate intervention strategies?
     - How is process management integrated with our design and improvement cycles?

- How do we deal with common cause or special cause variability?

- Does it feed into the process management approach?

Use a Process Management Chart (also known as a QC Process Chart) to communicate information about processes to your organization and track process progress. Also use a Process Management Chart to collect and analyze data during the pilot. Include the CTQs and the process and input measures related to the CTQs in your chart.

What is it?

The Process Management Chart summarizes the key information a process owner needs to effectively monitor and control a process (including the type of corrective action to take in response to signals from the measurement system).

Why use it?

To ensure that process owners in the organization have the information they need to maintain and control the design once it is implemented

How do I do it?

1. Create a chart with three columns: a "Plan/Do" column, a "Check" column, and an "Act" column.

2. Use a flowchart to fill in the Plan/Do column of the chart.

- Capture the essential steps of the process you designed. For each key step, show how the operation should be done or provide a reference to a document that describes the step.

Tip Use a Deployment Flowchart to document processes that flow across departments or areas. Use an Activity Flowchart to document processes where work is performed by one person or group.

3. Complete the Check column of the chart.

- Describe when and how you will collect data to monitor the processes and their outputs, (e.g., elapsed time, completeness, errors, or temperature).

- For each key process indicator, describe any important targets, tolerances, or specifications to which the process should conform if it is running well (e.g., eight hours from receipt, all boxes checked, 125°F–135°F). Use targets or specifications defined by customers, regulatory policies, or process knowledge as these standards.

- For each key process indicator, describe how the monitored data should be recorded (e.g., on a Checklist, Run Chart, Control Chart, or Scatter Diagram). Describe, if necessary, who will record the data and how.

Tip For manufacturing processes, describe any technical specifications that you have to meet. For administrative and service processes, describe the quality criteria defined for the process.

---

4. Complete the Act column of the chart.

- Describe how process owners or operators should react, depending on what they find as they measure the process.

- Address what you will do to control any damage that may occur in the process. Ask:

  - Who should do what with the output of the defective process?

  - What should be done for customers who receive the defective output?

  - What adjustments should we make to ensure that the defects do not occur again?

- Address the procedures you will use for any necessary process adjustments. Ask:

  - What must we do to gain sufficient under-standing of this process so that we know what adjustments and accommodations are routinely necessary to prevent a recurrence of this problem?

- Address the procedures you will use for process improvement.

  - Who in the organization needs what data in what form to be able to make sound decisions regarding new systems or reme-dies at deeper levels in the organization (i.e., changes in basic designs or policies)?

A Sample Process Management Chart

Plan/Do — Flowchart					Check	Act
Employee	Administrative Support	Human Resources	Financial Services	Management	Key Process Indicators	Corrective Actions
Incurs expense and does activity					100% inspection for standards: 1. Received by 5 p.m. Tues. (on-site) or 5 p.m. Wed. (by mail). 2. Operational definitions of expenses used. 3. Complete information provided. 4. Columns added and summary completed.	Correct form or return to employee. Discuss corrections with employee. Provide training if needed.
Completes white expense form and yellow timesheet	Receives form; checks coding of expenses					
	Copy to HR; copy saved for invoicing; original & yellow receipts to Financial Services	Records data — Prepares monthly report	Enters data into spreadsheet		Receipts behind form, stapled in upper left corner. HR does 100% inspection for proper use of time-coding vacation, leave, and holiday expenses used.	Correct form or return to employee. Discuss corrections with employee. Provide training if needed. If unclear about budget codes, check with manager.
		Resolve discrepancies	Correct? — No / Yes → Issue check	Management	FS responsible for: 1. All charges allocated. 2. Proper use of budget codes.	If incorrect: 1. Work with Administrative Support to resolve. 2. Track common areas of problems and report to manager monthly.

226 Design

©2004 GOAL/QPC

Once you have identified the process owners who will have ongoing responsibility for implementing, monitoring, and improving the design, update the change plan:

- Identify any new stakeholders (in operations management) and do a stakeholder commitment analysis.
- Review and update the communication plans.
- Integrate the organizational change plan with the pilot and implementation plans.

4.9 Review the Pre-Pilot Design

The pre-pilot design review is the last of many technical reviews conducted during the detailed design phase. It:

- Ensures that all of the elements of the design are complete.
- Ensures that all of the designed elements are well-integrated and that interfaces between different parts of the design are completely seamless.
- Identifies possible failure points and areas of vulnerability to be tested in the pilot.
- Reviews the pilot and implementation plans.
- Reviews the process management plans.

Note: Unlike the concept review where all interested parties are allowed to comment on the design, the pre-pilot review is usually restricted to technical discussions.

Because the design is more complex at this stage, the design review process itself becomes more complex.

For each critical design element, there may be multiple meetings before the final design review takes place, including (in sequence):

- Small group meetings to allow groups to review individual parts or modules of the design.

- Preliminary design review preparatory meetings to collect and review all necessary documentation, ensure consistency and completeness in analysis and reporting, and work on problems or issues that may affect the design review.

- Formal design review meetings.

After you review the designs for the individual elements, conduct a final pre-pilot review to inspect the overall design and to review the pilot plans and implementation plans before launching the pilot.

Note: All of the steps in the pre-pilot design review include feedback loops. Based on the results of the design review for a particular element, you may need to conduct another of series of preparatory meetings to address issues before you schedule the final pre-pilot review. Similarly, findings from the pre-pilot review may suggest corrections to the design of one or more elements (which will need to be reviewed again) before you can launch the pilot.

Feedback Loops
in the Pre-Pilot Design Review

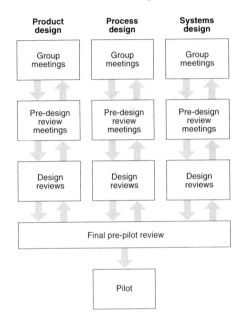

To keep the review process effective:

- Establish the review objectives and agenda in advance.
- Complete all pre-work in preparatory meetings.
- Keep the documentation clear and consistent.

- Index the documentation to make it easy to find and reference.

- Distribute the documentation in advance of the meeting.

- Set up follow-up procedures for confirming the completion of identified action items.

A successful design review requires preparation and planning. More than at any other stage in the design process, the consistency, accuracy, and readability of the documentation for this review can seriously impact the quality of the pre-pilot design review.

Give the participants enough time to read the documentation before the review session itself. Ask participants to submit questions in advance so that the design review process can flow smoothly. Also, clearly state the objectives of the review and ensure that they are understood by all parties so that there are no digressions or diversions that may impact the review's effectiveness.

Documents to use in a pre-pilot design review include:

- A description of the design, which could include models, prototypes, blueprints, diagrams, and specification lists.

- A description of all design tests and results, including Simulations, trial runs, FMEAs/EMEAs, and any other tests conducted on the design. (Be sure to provide all of the results with adequate supporting documentation and place special emphasis on identified high-risk elements or failure points.)

- A description of the range of conditions under which you will test the design, including details of how the pilot will test the design under these conditions. (Detail the legal and environmental issues that may impact the performance of the design as well.)

The output of the pre-pilot design review will include:

- A list of participants.
- A list of key issues raised, identifying who raised them.
- A list of proposed actions, including who is responsible for each action.
- A list of changes to reviewed documentation.
- A schedule of future meetings to assess the completion of proposed actions.
- A schedule of future design review meetings, as appropriate.

Completing the pre-pilot design review could lead you to:

- Redesign one or more elements of the design and move to the pilot.
- Redesign one or more elements of the design and schedule another design review.
- Move to pilot planning.

Clearly, the first two options apply if the design review indicates that there are issues with one or more elements of the design or if the design elements do not fit together. If you have not adequately prepared prior to the design review, you may find yourself faced with the second option, which will usually delay the launch date of the product or service. While this is still better than discovering errors after launch, this option is less efficient than the first option and could result in significant customer dissatisfaction due to the delay.

Note: For further information and examples of design reviews, refer to *Product Design Review—A Method for Error-Free Product Development*, Takeshi Ichida (ed.), Productivity Press, Portland, Oregon, 1996.

4.10 Hold a Tollgate Review

Note: For general information on tollgate reviews, see section 1.5 in the Define step.

The tollgate review for the Design step focuses on:

- The developed design.
- Completed Simulation or FMEA/EMEA analysis.
- Design solutions for vulnerable elements.
- Organizational change plan updates.
- Process management system variables and details.
- Plans for the pilot.

This tollgate review can lead you to:

- Redesign one or more elements.
- Look for alternate vendors if the chosen vendors do not provide the necessary results for the design.
- Improve the process management and/or pilot plan.
- Increase the duration of the pilot.
- Implement the pilot as planned.

How do I do it?

1. Update the Storyboard.
2. Review the Tollgate Review Form used at the end of the Analyze step. Revise and answer the specific questions that describe what was done in this step and what you need to do in the next step.

The Design Tollgate Review Form

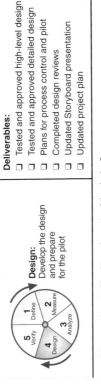

Design:
Develop the design and prepare for the pilot

Wheel diagram:
1 Define
2 Measure
3 Analyze
4 Design
5 Verify

Deliverables:

☐ Tested and approved high-level design
☐ Tested and approved detailed design
☐ Plans for process control and pilot
☐ Completed design reviews
☐ Updated Storyboard presentation
☐ Updated project plan

- What are the prioritized key elements of the design?
- How do the elements relate to meeting the CTQs?
- How was the design tested? What were the test results?
- How did you involve customers in the design evaluation?
- How did you identify vulnerabilities in the design? What were the vulnerabilities and how are you addressing these?
- What is your plan for conducting a pilot?
- What limitations or barriers have you encountered?
- Review your project plan: are you on track?
- What are your key learnings from the Design step?
- What are your next steps?

3. Present a progress report at the tollgate meeting using the Tollgate Review Form. Discuss the report and any issues; ask and answer questions about data and logic.

4. Identify the strengths and weaknesses of the project so far.

5. Decide on next steps.

6. Identify the strengths and weaknesses of the review.

Design
Verify Performance

Why do it?

To pilot and test the prototype, implement the final design, and close out the team.

Tools used in this step:

- Planning tools
- Data analysis tools:
  - Control Charts
  - Pareto Charts
- Standardization tools:
  - Flowcharts
  - Checklists
- Process Management Charts

Outputs of this step:

- A working prototype with documentation
- Plans for full implementation
- Control plans to help process owners measure, monitor, and maintain process capability
- A transition of ownership from the design team to management and the process owners/operators
- Completed project documentation and project closure
- A final tollgate review and updated Storyboard

Key questions answered in this step:

- How do we ensure that the pilot is realistic and produces meaningful results?

- What actions must we take if the performance of the pilot is unsatisfactory?

- How do we ensure that we can sustain the performance of a successful design over time?

- How do we reward the design team and celebrate their accomplishments?

- How can we share the lessons learned by the design team with the entire organization?

- How can we make sure that the organization embraces and supports the changes resulting from the design?

How do I do it?

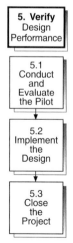

©2004 GOAL/QPC

5.1 Conduct and Evaluate the Pilot

1. **Use the Plan-Do-Check-Act (PDCA) Cycle as you conduct the pilot.**

Note: The implementation of a typical design will proceed through one or more turns of the PDCA Cycle. The initial turn is the pilot, which often leads to one or more improvement activities prior to full-scale implementation.

*   Make careful observations of all activities, effects, and interactions during the pilot. Be sure to continue the pilot long enough to establish reliable baseline performance data.

*   Pay close attention to the Check step of the PDCA Cycle when conducting and evaluating the pilot. Be sure to:

    -   Check both the pilot plan and the results.

    -   Compare the plan to what actually occurred. Ask:

        *   What changes in schedule occurred? Why?

        *   Were instructions followed? If not, why?

        *   How well did training and communication prepare people for the pilot? What improvements are needed to prepare them for full implementation?

        *   Were processes and procedures adequately documented? What checklists, visual cues, or

job aids would have helped? What improvements are needed?

- What unexpected barriers, issues, or rework occurred? What may have caused these problems? What remedies were tried? How successful were they? What improvements are needed?

Tip Pilots for complex projects should typically be 12–16 weeks long. Pilots for less complex projects should be 6–8 weeks long. Be sure to allow the process to stabilize for the first 2–3 weeks before collecting data.

Caution: Even a small process change can affect many other processes. Make sure the design does not cause problems for internal supplier and/or customer processes. Inform people in areas such as planning, inventory, facilities management, and quality control of any changes to allow them to adjust their work where necessary, and check administrative processes in personnel, finance, or accounting departments for unforeseen consequences.

2. **Use the pilot to check your process documentation.**

- Ask:

  - Are all procedures written clearly?

  - Is the process standardized at the right level of detail?

  - Can people follow the standards?

3. **Use the pilot to check your plans for ongoing process management once the design is fully implemented.**

- Ask:

  - What did we learn from the data collection during the pilot that will improve ongoing data collection for process management?

- When problems occurred during the pilot, was it clear to participants what actions to take? Could they take those actions?

- Do we need to update the process management plan?

4. **Use the Check and Act steps of the PDCA Cycle as a bridge between the pilot and full-scale implementation, and between implementation and ongoing process control.**

   • Compare the pilot results to the CTQs:

- Did all of the elements of the design perform as required? If not, why? What might have caused the variation?	*Check* step
- Is performance acceptable? How satisfied were pilot customers with the performance?	*Check* step
- If the pilot results are good, capture the learnings and prepare for full-scale implementation.	*Act* step
- If significant gaps are identified, conduct a root cause analysis to understand why.	*Act* step
- After modifying the design to address the root cause(s), consider conducting another pilot.	*Act* step
- Document all of your results, procedures, and learnings.	*Act* step

   • Be sure the organization can consistently achieve the results *because of* the design and not just occasionally *in spite of* the design due to heroic efforts.

Caution: Make sure that people are following the designed procedures; otherwise, the results of the pilot may not be the results of the design.

5. **Perform a pilot review.**

   - After you complete the pilot and analyze the data, review the results with management. Focus on:

     - Reviewing the analysis of pilot results (and re-pilot results as appropriate).

     - Discussing the problems identified during the pilot, causal analysis (identification and verification of the root cause[s]), and data on the effectiveness of countermeasures taken.

     - Reviewing any risk issues.

   - Review the performance of the pilot as compared to targets with key implementation managers/process owners and the team. Present data about the results and the plan. Present causal analysis along with proposed (and possibly tested) countermeasures. (At this point, there should be no "red light" risks and few moderate risks.) Create contingency plans for any remaining risks.

   - Discuss how well the communication and other organizational change strategies prepared participants in the pilot for their responsibilities.

   - Highlight what it will take to help the rest of the organization embrace and implement the new design. Review the current perspectives of stakeholders whose support is important to the design's success, along with plans to close any critical gaps.

   The results of the pilot review could lead you to:

   - Approve the design for full implementation and update any organizational change plans.

   - Request a redesign and retesting of all or parts of the design, along with another review.

Tip Use daily performance reviews when starting up the pilot and when you start up each stage of implementation; reduce their frequency as appropriate. Determine how you can:

- Have additional resources available to troubleshoot problems.
- Manage the expectations and perceptions of customers, management, staff, and stakeholders.
- Actively manage your implementation plan.
- Celebrate your successes.

6. **Verify the design's success.**

   Verifying a design's success is one of the last steps before making significant, sometimes irreversible investments. Make sure that everything is in order before moving on to full implementation of the design. Ask:

   - Is the process, product, or service meeting the performance requirements?
   - Are all process steps documented for a smooth transition?
   - Did we encounter implementation issues that we did not previously consider?

   Tip If you have validated and verified the design goals, you can then begin planning for full-scale implementation; if not, you should continue to use the PDCA Cycle until the design goals are met.

5.2 Implement the Design

Make sure that you involve other organizational leaders in reaffirming organizational ownership and responsibility for the full implementation of the design. A broad understanding and support for the design team's

---

boundaries is necessary for the transition to implementation to proceed smoothly.

> **Tip** Although the charter initially defined the full-scale implementation, you may have refined this definition in the Multistage Plan as the design evolved. Be sure to revisit prior agreements about the boundaries of the implementation so that the design team knows when its work is complete.

To implement the design:

1.	Select the implementation strategy.	*Plan* step
2.	Develop the implementation plans.	*Plan* step
3.	Update the documentation for procedures.	*Plan* step
4.	Update the process management plan.	*Plan* step
5.	Update the implementation plan FMEA/EMEA.	*Plan* step
6.	Carry out the implementation.	*Do* step
7.	Review the implementation.	*Check/Act* steps

5.2.1 Select the implementation strategy

How do I do it?

1. **Identify how you will implement the design in different locations or areas.**

   • You can implement the design:

     - In sequence (i.e., implement the design in one location before starting the next location).

- In phases (i.e., partially implement the design at one location, then start a second location).
- All-at-once (i.e., start all locations simultaneously).

You can also combine these approaches.

To help you decide which approach to use to implement the design, consider:

- What resources the approach will need.
- How it will affect ongoing work and your ability to meet commitments.
- How long it will take to complete the implementation.
- How it will affect other initiatives that are under way.
- What technology issues you will encounter as you implement this approach.

5.2.2 Develop the implementation plans

How do I do it?

1. **Create detailed work plans.**
   - Use the pilot plans as the foundation for the detailed work plans.
   - Include all of the tasks needed to bring the new process, product, or service up to full capability.
   - Incorporate scale-up plans (for issues that will arise when moving from a limited trial to full-scale implementation) and improvements from the pilot.
   - Have the people involved in the implementation participate in creating the plan so it is tailored to their situation.

- Include opportunities for employees in different areas to customize the plans for their particular environment. (Participation in tailoring the plans encourages support from a broad base of employees, and this support is needed for a successful design.)

- If necessary, use subplans for each design element (e.g., a facilities implementation plan, an information systems implementation plan, etc.).

2. **Create a transition plan if the new design will replace existing work processes, equipment, or facilities.**

- Minimize the disruption that the new design could cause by creating a plan to facilitate the transition to the new design. Describe how the organization's ongoing work will be handled while the new design is being installed. Common approaches to minimize disruption and transition the work include:

  - Shutting down the current location and transferring the work elsewhere until the changeover to the new system is complete.

  - Running both old and new systems in parallel until the new system is stable.

  - Using rapid methods for transferring work from the old system to the new system during low capacity times.

3. **Update the training plan used in the pilot.**

- Include:

  - A list of the information that you need to share.

  - A plan to develop the materials used in training.

  - A description of the audience for the training and an assessment of their training needs.

  - A plan for how you will spread the training to the appropriate people in the organization.

  - A plan to test the effectiveness of the training.

©2004 GOAL/QPC

Carefully coordinate the training plan to coincide with the rest of the implementation plan. Include relevant process maps, procedures, and documentation. (Update and prepare the standard work practices prior to the beginning of training.) Also remember that you may need ongoing implementation support or a help desk to supplement some training situations.

Check the training plan for completeness. Ask:

- What steps or activities will change as a result of the new design?

- Who performs these steps or activities? What is the best way to prepare these people to do the work to support the new design?

- Is training needed? If so, what materials do we need?

- Who can conduct the training? What preparation will they need?

- When will we deliver the training? Where?

- How will we follow-up or support the training?

- How will we evaluate the training?

4. **Update the communication plan used in the pilot.**
   - Include:
     - An explanation of the business case for the new process, product, or service.
     - A report on the pilot and what made it successful.
     - A "What's In It For Me?" analysis.
     - A description of how company leadership will support the effort.
     - A review of the implementation and training plan.

While ongoing communication is important throughout the design, pay special attention to how you plan to communicate the implementation of the new design to the organization, to customers, and to stakeholders outside of the organization.

Closely coordinate the timing of the communication plan with the implementation plans so that customers do not expect the new process, product, or service before it is available, and investors do not expect to see the results from the new process, product, or service sooner than is reasonable.

5. **Form implementation teams at each location.**
   • These teams will help:
     - Adapt the draft implementation plan to their location.
     - Carry out the implementation at their location.
     - Help employees at the location change work habits and methods to support the new process, product, or service.
     - Report progress and problems to management and to the design team (until the design team is closed).

5.2.3 Update the documentation for the procedures

How do I do it?

1. **Update documented standard operating procedures (based on the results of the pilot) and distribute the updated procedures.**
   • Include flowcharts, drawings, schematics, written instructions, and cautions.

- Make sure that documentation is at an appropriate level of detail (i.e., it is specific in telling precisely what actions to take and when and where to take them). Make sure it describes how to prevent variation (i.e., it describes underlying cause-and-effect relationships) and focuses on priorities.

  Note: Documentation may be written, photographed, illustrated, or on video or audio tape.

- Record what to do and why, in language that is simple enough for most people unfamiliar with the job to follow and produce the desired results.

  Tip You will likely need documentation for each design element (e.g., documentation for sales, order processing, manufacturing, shipping, customer service, technical support, etc.).

- Store the documented standard operating procedures so that:

  - Everyone has easy access to the information.

  - You can easily update them.

  - You can easily control versions of the documentation.

  - You can have links between documents.

  - People who are not fully trained can easily use them.

  Tip Many organizations already have standard methods in place for documenting detailed work procedures. Use your organization's standard methods, if possible.

Sample Documentation for an Order Entry Process

Sales Dept.	Operational Documentation	Page 1 of 1	Picture - Flowchart - Drawing - Form - Etc.

Process Analysis Worksheet

Date: March 2   **Process:** Order Entry/Phone   **Owner:** Judy/Sales

Step	Major Step	Key Point	Special Instructions
	Take order by phone	1. Use order form	1. In file rack – First slot

	Complete form	1. Customer information	1. Customer key number
			  – Date
			  – Initials of order taker

		2. Payment method	2. Purchase order number
			  – Credit card information
			  – Tax status

		3. Marketing information	3. Buyer's name
			  – How they heard about the product
			  – What their company does

		4. Invoicing address	4. Invoice mailing address
			  – Fill in complete address
			  – Attention to whom?
			  – Phone number

		5. Shipping address	5. Shipping address
			  – Fill in complete address
			  – Attention to whom?
			  – Phone number

5.2.4 Update the process management plan

How do I do it?

1. **Base the plan for ongoing process management on the Process Management Chart developed in the Design step and tested in the pilot.**

    • Include:

      - A clarification of the process roles and a plan for who will fill those roles.

      - A working version of the Process Management Chart with the major process steps, measures, and response plans included.

      - A working version of the measurement and monitoring systems that you will use to manage the process on an ongoing basis, including what you will measure and how you will track it.

      - A schedule for process reviews.

2. **Use data analysis tools to monitor ongoing performance.**

    • To analyze the data from the Process Management Chart on an ongoing basis, have process owners monitor key measures to ensure that the performance level continues to meet requirements, and use appropriate charts (like a Control Chart) to display and analyze this data.

    Note: An in-depth discussion of Control Charts is beyond the scope of this book. For more information, see *The Memory Jogger™ II.*

A Sample Process Management Chart

The plan for doing the work — Flowchart				Checking the work — Key process indicators	Response to results — Corrective actions
Employee	Administrative Support	Human Resources	Financial Services	Management		

The plan for doing the work Flowchart	Checking the work Key process indicators	Response to results Corrective actions
Employee: Incurs expense and does activity. Completes white expense form and yellow timesheet.	100% inspection for standards: 1. Received by 5 p.m. Tues. (on-site) or 5 p.m. Wed. (by mail). 2. Operational definitions of expenses used. 3. Complete information provided. 4. Columns added and summary completed.	Correct form or return to employee. Discuss corrections with employee. Provide training if needed.
Administrative Support: Receives form; checks coding of expenses. Copy to Human Resources; copy saved for invoicing; original & receipts to Financial Services.	Receipts behind form, stapled in upper left corner.	Correct form or return to employee. Discuss corrections with employee. Provide training if needed.
Human Resources: Records data. Prepares monthly report.	Human Resources does 100% inspection for proper use of time coding, vacation, leave, and holiday expenses used.	If unclear about budget codes, check with manager.
Financial Services: Enters data into spreadsheet. Correct? No → Resolve discrepancies. Yes → Issue check.	Financial Services responsible for: 1. All charges allocated. 2. Proper use of budget codes.	If incorrect: 1. Work with Administrative Support to resolve. 2. Track common areas of problems and report to manager monthly.

A Sample Control Chart to Display Performance Data

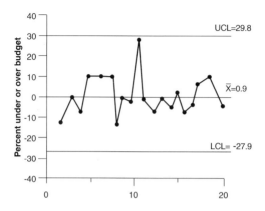

- Before using charts to monitor ongoing performance, decide:

  - Who will collect the data.

  - Who will plot the data.

  - Who will interpret the chart.

  - What they should do if a signal of special cause appears.

  - Where you will post the chart.

  - Whether you will create the chart by hand or on computer.

- Decide who will be responsible for the upkeep of the charts and for reacting to any signals. Make sure that everyone involved in using the chart has been trained to collect and plot the data, and understands special cause and common cause variation.

5.2.5 Update the implementation plan FMEA/EMEA

Because implementation and transition plans are complex, you must have a plan to minimize potential problems and take actions to minimize the likelihood of those problems. Analyze the pilot to identify new sources of failure or error, and continue to use the FMEA/EMEA to identify steps where problems are likely to occur and where the consequences of problems are serious.

As you develop contingency plans to minimize the likelihood of problems, consider:

- Developing communication plans to combat mis-understandings.
- Developing or revising key documentation so that critical plan steps are identified and understood.
- Making key process steps error-proof.
- Adding additional or more-skilled resources to vulnerable steps along the critical path.

5.2.6 Carry out the implementation

Use the PDCA Cycle, just as you did in the pilot, to implement the design.

5.2.7 Review the implementation

Complex implementations may require a final review *after* you begin to roll-out the design but *before* you close the project. This review ensures that the organization is prepared to assume responsibility for continued roll-out and ongoing monitoring of the design.

How do I do it?

1. Review any problems encountered during implementation, analyze the causes, and identify any efforts to remedy the problems.

2. Analyze any performance gaps and address efforts to close the gaps.

3. Revise the plans for continued roll-out and monitoring.

5.3 Close the Project

How do I do it?

1. Transition the responsibilities for the implemented design to management and the process owners/operators, and communicate the results of the design project throughout the organization.

   • Communicating the project results helps the design team and the organization recognize when the design project is completed and on-going responsibility for maintaining the performance has shifted to the process owners in various operations.

2. Once you have transitioned the responsibilities for implementation, complete a formal closure process that:

   • Captures the lessons learned about the design process.

   • Communicates the project's ending.

   • Recognizes the considerable time and effort that went into the initiative.

   Tip Some design projects never seem to end. Often this is because the organization is unprepared to assume its responsibilities for ongoing project management, which, with some designs, can take considerable time. Sometimes the team is reluctant to leave the new design in the hands of ongoing operations. Sometimes both the organization and the team are simply unclear about when the team's responsibilities are fulfilled.

It is important to have a clear closure to a project, even if the same design team is to work on the next generation of the design.

5.3.1 Capture the lessons learned about the design process

1. **Capture, compile, and share the lessons learned in the design process so that current and future design projects can leverage and apply them.**

   • Capture learnings:

     - About your results.

     - About the design process:

       • What you learned about the design process that surprised you.

       • What you learned about conducting a design project.

       • What advice you would give to other teams.

       • What helped your team and what hindered it.

       • What worked and what didn't.

     - About the team's functioning:

       • What you learned about working on a team.

       • How well your team worked together.

       • How well you worked with a sponsor and reviewers.

2. **Use a final tollgate review to capture the lessons learned.**

   • Update the Storyboard.

   • Present a progress report at the tollgate meeting using the Tollgate Review Form.

The Verify Tollgate Review Form

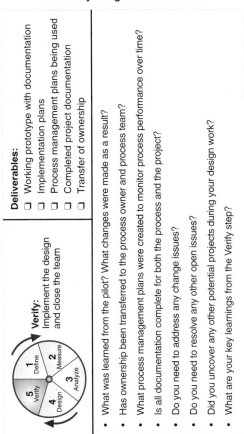

Verify:
Implement the design and close the team

Deliverables:

- ❏ Working prototype with documentation
- ❏ Implementation plans
- ❏ Process management plans being used
- ❏ Completed project documentation
- ❏ Transfer of ownership

- What was learned from the pilot? What changes were made as a result?
- Has ownership been transferred to the process owner and process team?
- What process management plans were created to monitor process performance over time?
- Is all documentation complete for both the process and the project?
- Do you need to address any change issues?
- Do you need to resolve any other open issues?
- Did you uncover any other potential projects during your design work?
- What are your key learnings from the Verify step?

- Discuss the progress report and any issues that arose; ask and answer questions about data and logic.
- Identify the project's strengths and weaknesses.
- Identify the review's strengths and weaknesses.

5.3.2 Communicate the project's ending

Join with the project team and its sponsor(s) in communicating the team's results to the organization. Include:

- What the team accomplished.
- The impact on the organization.
- Which employees could benefit from the lessons learned.
- The best method to communicate the lessons learned.

5.3.3 Recognize the time and effort that went into the initiative

Select an appropriate way to celebrate closure and determine how you will close the team.

> **Tip** Recognition is an important part of celebration and should reinforce intrinsic sources of satisfaction and motivation.

Additional Resources

Web-based sources of information

www.isixsigma.com
Solely dedicated to Six Sigma; excellent source of free information on all facets of Six Sigma.

www.pdma.org
Site for the Product Development and Management Organization; has an especially helpful glossary of terms.

www.asmsup.com
Site for the American Supplier Institute; excellent source for Taguchi Methods and Quality Function Deployment.

www.sei.cmu.edu
Site for the Software Engineering Institute (SEI); source of the Capability Maturity Model for software development.

www.aiag.org
Site for the Automotive Industry Action Group; excellent source of information on the automotive Production Part Approval Process (PPAP).

www.triz-journal.com
Site dedicated to providing information about "Theory of Inventive Problem Solving," (TRIZ) developed by Genrich Altshuller; contains articles and case studies.

Text-based sources of information

For more information on:	Refer to:
Brainstorming and Brainwriting	*The Creativity Tools Memory Jogger™* or *The Idea Edge*
Control Charts	*The Memory Jogger™ II*
Creative Confrontation Methods	*The Creativity Tools Memory Jogger™*
Creativity Tools	*The Creativity Tools Memory Jogger™*, *The Idea Edge*, or *Product Design: Fundamentals and Methods* by N.J.M. Roozenburg, J. Eekels, and N.F.M.Roozenburg, John Wiley & Sons
Data Analysis Tools	*The Six Sigma Memory Jogger™ II*
Design of Experiments	*The Six Sigma Memory Jogger™ II* or *The Black Belt Memory Jogger™*

Continued on next page

For more information on:	Refer to:
Design Reviews	*Product Design Review—A Method for Error-Free Product Development*, Takeshi Ichida (editor), Productivity Press
Design Scorecards	*Design for Six Sigma: A Roadmap for Product Development* by Kai Yang and Basem El-Haik, McGraw-Hill
Flowcharts	*The Memory Jogger™ II*
Morphological Box	*The Creativity Tools Memory Jogger™* or *The Idea Edge*
Performance Functions (y = f (x))	*The Black Belt Memory Jogger™*
Process Analysis Tools	*The Six Sigma Memory Jogger™ II*
Project Management Tools	*Project Management Memory Jogger™* or *The Six Sigma Memory Jogger™ II*
Project Planning Tools	*Project Management Memory Jogger™* or *The Six Sigma Memory Jogger™ II*
Pugh Matrix	*The Idea Edge*
Rolled Throughput Yield	*The Black Belt Memory Jogger™*
Run Charts	*The Memory Jogger™ II*
Scatter Diagrams	*The Memory Jogger™ II*
Selecting and Sorting Customer Statements	*Voices into Choices: Acting on the Voice of the Customer* by Gary Burchill and Christina Hepner Brodie, Oriel Incorporated
Sigma Values	*The Black Belt Memory Jogger™*
Standardization Tools	*The Six Sigma Memory Jogger™ II*
Storyboards	*The Six Sigma Memory Jogger™ II* or *The Problem Solving Memory Jogger™*
TRIZ	*Design for Six Sigma: A Roadmap for Product Development* by Kai Yang and Basem El-Haik, McGraw-Hill; or GOAL/QPC Research Report, *TRIZ: An Approach to Systematic Innovation*
Uncovering Customer Needs	"Want to Perfect Your Company's Service? Use Behavioral Science" by Richard B. Chase and Sriram Dasu, *Harvard Business Review*, June 2001

Unless noted otherwise, all resources are GOAL/QPC publications.

Storyboard

Note: The information in this section is adapted from
The Six Sigma Memory Jogger™ II.

What is it?

The Storyboard is a graphical or pictorial record of your
design project to help you track data, decisions, and
actions.

Why use it?

- To facilitate decision making
- To help maintain forward momentum
- To help prevent rework
- To provide a quick, visual summary of a team's
  work

Note: You can also use the elements of a Storyboard
as presentation materials. Many organizations keep
Storyboards permanently on record so that employees can have access to other team's work.

How do I do it?

1. **Maintain records throughout the life of your
   project.**

   - Agendas and meeting notes provide a permanent
     record of what issues are discussed at meetings–
     particularly what "to do" items you generated
     and what decisions you reached.

   - Records of customer interviews or surveys provide
     verbal data that will help to shape your effort.

Management, sponsors, or others in the organization might find this data helpful to use for future efforts.

- Data-collection sheets provide the source for your analysis. Keep them at least until the project is completed.

- Plans help you identify the components of a task, track your progress, and communicate your progress to others. Documented plans help you evaluate whether you did what you intended to do; they can also provide the basis for standardized work plans.

- Data charts help you understand your data, enable you to compare the outcome of the design effort with the initial situation, and provide a baseline for monitoring the process and making future improvements.

2. Create a Storyboard.

- Develop a pictorial record of the design steps by using the template on the following pages.

Tip Keep your text brief, use a lot of graphics, and make sure your graphics effectively communicate your message.

3. Present your Storyboard to others.

Organizations often ask design project participants to introduce others in the organization to new concepts, explain a concept or tool they used, and present examples of their applications of various concepts and tools. This is often done as a formal presentation.

Storyboard Template

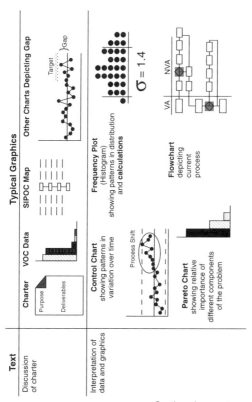

Typical Graphics

Charter — Purpose, Deliverables

VOC Data

SIPOC Map

Other Charts Depicting Gap — Target, Gap

Control Chart showing patterns in variation over time — Process Shift

Frequency Plot (Histogram) showing patterns in distribution and **calculations** — $\sigma = 1.4$

Pareto Chart showing relative importance of different components of the problem

Flowchart depicting current process — VA, NVA

Text

Discussion of charter

Interpretation of data and graphics

Continued on next page

Storyboard Template (cont.)

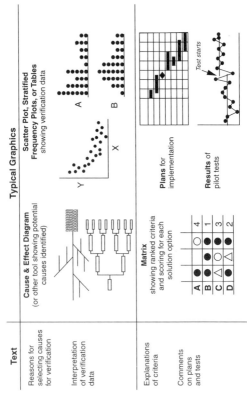

Typical Graphics

Scatter Plot, Stratified Frequency Plots, or Tables showing verification data

Cause & Effect Diagram (or other tool showing potential causes identified)

Plans for implementation

Test starts

Results of pilot tests

Matrix showing ranked criteria and scoring for each solution option

Text

Reasons for selecting causes for verification

Interpretation of verification data

Explanations of criteria

Comments on plans and tests

Continued on next page

Storyboard Template (cont.)

Text	Typical Graphics
Interpretation of analysis of results and methods	**Before and After Data** Comparing results with data previously collected. Plots drawn to same scale. 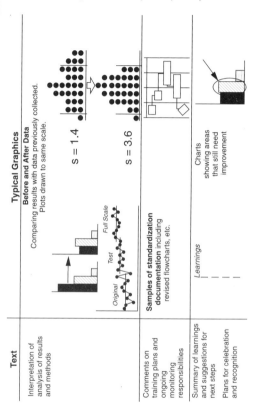 s = 1.4 s = 3.6
Comments on training plans and ongoing monitoring responsibilities	**Samples of standardization documentation** including revised flowcharts, etc.
Summary of learnings and suggestions for next steps Plans for celebration and recognition	Charts showing areas that still need improvement

Sigma Conversion Chart

Long-term Yield	Long-term Sigma	Short-term Sigma	Defects per Million
99.99966%	4.5	6.0	3.4
99.9995%	4.4	5.9	5
99.9992%	4.3	5.8	8
99.9990%	4.2	5.7	10
99.9980%	4.1	5.6	20
99.9970%	4.0	5.5	30
99.9960%	3.9	5.4	40
99.9930%	3.8	5.3	70
99.9900%	3.7	5.2	100
99.9850%	3.6	5.1	150
99.9770%	3.5	5.0	230
99.9670%	3.4	4.9	330
99.9520%	3.3	4.8	480
99.9320%	3.2	4.7	680
99.9040%	3.1	4.6	960
99.8650%	3.0	4.5	1,350
99.8140%	2.9	4.4	1,860
99.7450%	2.8	4.3	2,550
99.6540%	2.7	4.2	3,460
99.5340%	2.6	4.1	4,660
99.3790%	2.5	4.0	6,210
99.1810%	2.4	3.9	8,190
98.930%	2.3	3.8	10,700
98.610%	2.2	3.7	13,900
98.220%	2.1	3.6	17,800
97.730%	2.0	3.5	22,700
97.130%	1.9	3.4	28,700
96.410%	1.8	3.3	35,900
95.540%	1.7	3.2	44,600
94.520%	1.6	3.1	54,800
93.320%	1.5	3.0	66,800
91.920%	1.4	2.9	80,800
90.320%	1.3	2.8	96,800
88.50%	1.2	2.7	115,000
86.50%	1.1	2.6	135,000
84.20%	1.0	2.5	158,000
81.60%	0.9	2.4	184,000
78.80%	0.8	2.3	212,000
75.80%	0.7	2.2	242,000
72.60%	0.6	2.1	274,000
69.20%	0.5	2.0	308,000
65.60%	0.4	1.9	344,000
61.80%	0.3	1.8	382,000
58.00%	0.2	1.7	420,000
54.00%	0.1	1.6	460,000
50.00%	0.0	1.5	500,000
46.00%	-0.1	1.4	540,000
42.00%	-0.2	1.3	580,000
38.00%	-0.3	1.2	620,000
34.00%	-0.4	1.1	660,000
31.00%	-0.5	1.0	690,000
27.00%	-0.6	0.9	730,000
24.00%	-0.7	0.8	760,000

Note: The 1.5 sigma shift is included in this chart.

Notes

Notes